Life
Without
LIGHT

A Journey to Earth's Dark Ecosystems

MELISSA STEWART

Foreword by Lynn Margulis and Dorion Sagan

A VENTURE BOOK

FRANKLIN WATTS

A Division of Grolier Publishing

NEW YORK   LONDON   HONG KONG   SYDNEY   DANBURY, CONNECTICUT

Photographs ©: Archive Photos: 21; Corbis-Bettmann: 34, 101 UPI); Cristian Lascu: 70 (Gess-Romania); ENP Images: 67 (Gerry Ellis); NASA: 111 (U. S. Geological Survey, Flagstaff, AZ); NOAA Department of Commerce: 42; Peter Girguis: 28, 47, 49; Photo Researchers: 90 (Archive), 109 (Fletcher & Baylis), 92 (Biophoto Assoc.), 26 (Peter David), 11 (Lincoln Nutting/National Audubon Society), 113 (Nasa/Science Sources), 39 (C. Seghers), 9 (Blair Seltz), 99 (Jim Steinberg); Richard A. Lutz: 52; Serban Sarbu: 75 (Gess-Romania); Southwest Texas State University: 80, 84; Superstock, Inc.: 65 (National Gallery, London/ Bridgeman Art Library, London); Verena Tunnicliffe: 56, 59 (University of Victoria, BC.); Wildlife Conservation Society, headquartered at the Bronx Zoo: 19; Woods Hole Oceanographic Institution: 22 (Rod Catanach).

Insert #1 photographs ©: Cristian Lascu: 6, 7 (Gess-Romania); Photo Researchers: 12 (Joseph T. Collins), 2 (Jim W. Grace), 5 (Charles E. Mohr), 3 (John Serrao), 13 (Dr. Kari Lounatmaa/SPL); Serban Sarbu: 8, 9, 10; Southwest Texas State University: 11; Visuals Unlimited: 4 (Nathan W. Cohen), 1 (Richard Thom).

Insert #2 photographs ©: NOAA Department of Commerce: 7; Peter Girguis: 3, 6; Photo Researchers: 2 (Dr. Fred Espenak/SPL); Shana Goffredi: 9 (University of California, Santa Barbara, CA.); U.S. Geological Survey, Denver, CO: 1; Verena Tunnicliffe: 8 (University of Victoria, BC.); Visuals Unlimited: 10 (Whoi-D. Foster), 4 (Robert Degoursey), 5 (Ken Lucas).

Illustrations by Bob Italiano

Visit Franklin Watts on the internet at:
http://publishing.grolier.com

Library of Congress Cataloging-in-Publication Data

Stewart, Melissa
    Life without light: a journey to Earth's dark ecosytems / Melissa Stewart.
        p. cm. — (A Venture book)
    Includes bibliographical references and index.
    Summary: Explores some of the world's most unusual ecosystems found in caves, the deep sea, hydrothermal vents on the ocean floor, underground aquifers, and rock deep below Earth's surface.
    ISBN 0-531-11529-1 (lib. bdg.)   0-531-15972-8 (pbk.)
    1. Biotic communities—Juvenile literature. 2. Habitat (Ecology)—Juvenile literature. 3. Life—Origin—Juvenile literature. 4. Life (Biology)—Juvenile literature. [1. Biotic communities. 2. Habitat (Ecology) 3. Life—Origin. 4. Life (Biology)] I. Title.
QH541.14.S755   1999
577—dc21   97-35341
                                                                 CIP
                                                                  AC

Acknowledgments

In many ways this book is a culmination of everything I have ever learned about biology, earth science, and chemistry, with a little bit of space science thrown in. It's difficult to thank a lifetime full of people who have offered me support and encouragement.

At the top of my list are, of course, my parents and brother. Other names that come to mind include Susannah Tracy Touchet, David Wachtel and Lisa Plotnik, my classmates at SERP, the Grolier lunch bunch, and Glyn Lipham.

Special thanks are also deserved by Professor Karen Williams who encouraged me to be anything but a doctor and opened many doors for me. I must also thank the experts who reviewed this book: Janann V. Jenner, Ph.D.; Cindy Lee Van Dover, Ph.D., Institute of Marine Science, University of Alaska Fairbanks; and Margaret Caruthers, Ph.D., Department of Earth and Planetary Science, American Museum of Natural History, New York.

No words can express my gratitude to Dr. Lynn Margulis, Distinguished University Professor at the University of Massachusetts and Dorion Sagan, her co-author, for reviewing the manuscript and writing a forward for this book.

I am also greatly indebted to Kathy Santini—the kindest person I've ever known—for making this book a reality.

Finally, I would like to thank my editor, Brendan January, for his steadfast support and guidance, his intelligence, and his friendship.

Foreword

All life requires light. Until recently, this statement was taken for granted by everyone, even scientists. But in the last 20 years, strange and fascinating new kinds of life have been discovered— pale cave-dwelling animals with sealed eyelids, blind catfish swimming in water supplies, and blood-red headless worms waving in the bubbling heat spewed from vents on the ocean floor. In this book, science journalist Melissa Stewart describes some of the strangest beings on Earth and makes a startling claim: life can make its own food and grow in complex communities in total darkness.

This discovery challenges the fundamental way we have traditionally viewed our sunny world and star-filled universe. By considering the idea that life exists without light, we may soon find the answers of questions that have baffled us for centuries: What are the limits to life? Does all life on Earth share the same common ancestor? Might life exist elsewhere in the universe?

A biologist who pursued writing because she did not want to limit herself, Stewart shows in this book the power of wide horizons. She focuses on places previously thought to be uninhabitable. She recounts how curious explorers and scientists discovered unique and intriguing ecosystems teeming with life—wierd animals that live in Texan wells, ancient bacteria that thrive in Yellowstone's bubbling muds and need the scorching heat of the hot springs, rare kinds of life embedded in rocks thousands of feet below the ground we walk on. These environments, remote and hostile to us, are home-sweet-home for them.

Unfamiliar habitats invite us to question the world we live in and the very nature of life itself. Whereas "the truth is out there" may be the catchy phrase of the popular television show *The X-Files*, *Life Without Light* shows that the truth is actually in here—in the recently discovered black smoking bubbles rising from the bottom of the sea and in the thriving communities in the watery cracks in Earth's hardest rocks.

This book is an informative and exciting look at the bizarre and peculiar hidden beings recently uncovered by modern science. It is inspired by potential answers these creatures may provide to some of humanity's oldest questions. To enjoy the "dark side" of life, we encourage students and teachers to take a close look at Melissa Stewart's *Life Without Light*.

Lynn Margulis and Dorion Sagan

Contents

Introduction

Thousands of feet below Earth's surface live some of the most unusual creatures imaginable. They exist in total darkness and get the energy they need to live from a chemical reaction that requires nothing more than water and rock. According to some scientists, these microbes may be as closely related to fossil-like material recently discovered in a meteorite from Mars as they are to any creature living on Earth today. Scientists around the world are fascinated by these bizarre creatures for a very important reason—if they didn't exist, we might not either.

By studying these mysterious microbes and similar creatures found at the bottom of the ocean and in swamps, hot springs, and the digestive tracts of some animals, researchers hope to answer some of the most basic questions in science. These creatures could help us discover where, when, and how life originated. Scientists could also learn how early life survived and evolved on Earth. Ultimately, we hope to find out if life exists only on Earth, or if there are hundreds, thousands, or even millions of galaxies with planets containing life.

Are we alone in the universe? Are we unique? These are questions that have been asked ever since humans, or perhaps even our prehuman ancestors, have had the ability to wonder about all those shining lights in the night sky.

Stunning discoveries made in the last few years seem to have brought us closer than ever to the answers. Modern scientists would be unable to recognize the significance of these recent discoveries, however, if it weren't for the massive body of scientific knowledge accumulated by countless hardworking scientists over the course of several centuries.

These early scientists began looking at the world by studying the environments closest at hand—the forests, fields, and wetlands. Next, scientists concentrated their efforts on lakes and ponds, rivers and streams, the seashore, and coral reefs. Their research showed that all these ecosystems operate according to the same basic set of rules. One of these rules is that each habitat's ultimate energy source is the Sun.

In the last 50 years, scientists have begun to explore some of the world's most remote ecosystems. This book takes you on a journey to some of these places—caves, the deep sea, hydrothermal vents on the ocean floor, underground aquifers, and rock buried deep below Earth's surface.

Each time scientists encounter a new habitat, they find surprises—creatures with bizarre features and unusual behaviors. More importantly, they have come to realize that these habitats do not always follow the same rules as more familiar ecosystems. When scientists ask themselves questions like "What is life?" and "What conditions are necessary for life?" they are often amazed by the answers.

At one time, sunlight was at the top of scientists' list of necessities. This is no longer true. In fact, researchers have found that Earth's array of organisms is so diverse and adaptable that it requires surprisingly little to survive. In general, creatures in each environment seem to make do with whatever resources are available.

CHAPTER ONE

The Light of Day

There is nothing new under the Sun.

Ecclesiastes 1:9

As dawn breaks, a red-winged blackbird shakes itself awake, flies to its favorite cattail, and lets out a loud, shrill call: "Cuck-la-reee." From this perch, the blackbird can inspect its entire territory and look across to the opposite shore of the small, secluded lake it returns to every year.

It is early spring, and the bird is looking for a mate. "Cuck-la-reee!" The bird delivers another slurred, vibrating call to let any nearby females know its location.

As the morning passes, clouds meander across the bright blue sky. The shape of each is mirrored on the calm surface of the water below. Suddenly, the sky darkens as the Sun's

This great blue heron
has just caught
a large fish.

light is momentarily blocked by the body of a huge, awk-wardly beautiful bird flying overhead. The lanky bird glides gracefully above the lake, slowly flapping its massive wings and dragging its long, sticklike legs behind.

From high above, the great blue heron surveys the lake for the perfect fishing spot. It watches for fish surfacing in search of their morning meal of insects. The heron is looking for a breakfast of its own.

The great bird lands in a small cove and silently wades through the shallow water. When it spots a potential victim, the heron extends its folded neck and stabs the unsuspecting fish with its long, spearlike bill. The bird devours its catch quickly.

A moment later the heron shakes out its wings and transforms its body into a lean, perfectly erect pole. As the bird suns itself among the cove's tall reeds, it is invisible to its enemies. A careful observer might just catch a glimpse of water on the heron's bill, as it gleams in the morning Sun.

The cove's water is stagnant, and the surface is covered with a mat of duckweed. These tiny plants take advantage of the Sun's early morning rays, too. They are making the materials their bodies need to grow and reproduce using a process called *photosynthesis.*

Photosynthesis is a complex chemical reaction. For this reaction to take place, plants like duckweed need to have access to water, H_2O, and a gas called carbon dioxide, CO_2, which is abundant in the air. The reaction is powered by energy captured from the Sun. Photosynthesis produces a simple sugar called glucose, $C_6H_{12}O_6$, and oxygen, O_2.

Duckweed is not the only organism busy photosynthesizing. All green plants and algae spend the day carrying out this important chemical reaction. Some bacteria photosynthesize, too. (As you will learn later, some kinds of bacteria carry out a different type of photosynthesis. They rely on a chemical called *hydrogen sulfide* instead of water. Oxygen is not a product of this reaction.)

On top of the duckweed mat are thousands of colonies of tiny organisms called *Gloeotrichia. Gloeotrichia* is a type of *cyanobacteria,* or blue-green algae. Each colony of *Gloeotrichia*— which is shaped like a dandelion puffball—is made up of hundreds of microscopic creatures. An entire colony of *Gloeotrichia* is no more than 0.4 inches (1 cm) in diameter.

Both the *Gloeotrichia* and the duckweed are important sources of food for animals living in the lake. As mallards and wood ducks cruise around the lake, they nip at aquatic plants

and algae growing on top of and beneath the water's surface. Small fish also eat a variety of aquatic plants and algae, as well as cyanobacteria.

Plants, algae, and cyanobacteria are at the bottom of the lake's *food chain.* At the base of every ecosystem's food chain are *autotrophs.* This word has Greek origins; the first part—auto—means "self," and the second part—troph—means "nourishment." Thus, autotrophs—such as peach trees, petunias, and pines—do not rely on other living things for food. Autotrophs that get the energy they need from sunlight are called *photoautotrophs.* (In Greek, photo means "light.")

All autotrophs convert energy from their surroundings into a form they can use to build their own bodies and reproduce. Duckweed and other green plants store the energy they

Duckweed often covers the surface of stagnant ponds.

obtain from photosynthesis in simple sugars called *carbohydrates*. These sugars can be linked together into long chains called complex carbohydrates or *polysaccharides*. One important polysaccharide is starch.

When you eat a potato, you are actually eating the fleshy root of a potato plant. This root is made mostly of starch. Starch is an important part of your diet. In fact, two-thirds of all calories consumed by humans throughout the world come from the starch in plants such as rice, wheat, and corn.

Any organism that relies on other living things for food is called a *heterotroph*, which means "other nourishment." All animals are heterotrophs. They eat other creatures to get the materials they need to grow and reproduce. Animals can also be described as *chemoheterotrophs* because they get the energy they need from the chemicals in the bodies of the organisms they eat.

Many animals eat only plants. Horses, cows, deer, and zebras are all plant eaters, or *herbivores*. When an herbivore such as a zebra eats a plant such as grass, only about 10 percent of the energy stored in the plant's molecules can be used by the herbivore to build and maintain its own body. The rest of the energy is lost during the processes that convert plant material into the structures that make up the zebra's cells.

When a lion eats a zebra, only about 10 percent of the energy stored in the zebra's molecules is transferred to the molecules that make up the lion's body. This means that the lion can use only about 1 percent of the energy originally captured from the Sun by grass to build its own body.

So if a lion has such a hard time getting energy, how does this ferocious cat muster enough strength to be the king of the jungle? It's simple—a lion eats a lot of zebras, not to mention impalas, wildebeest, and their kin. And when these animals are in short supply, lions will set their sights on rodents, birds, turtles, lizards, fish, and even ostrich eggs.

A hungry lion can eat up to one-quarter of its body weight in one sitting. On the African plains, there are about a thousand zebras, impalas, and wildebeest for every lion. No ecosystem in the world can support as many meat eaters, or *carnivores,* as herbivores. If the population of carnivores begins to grow too large, some will starve to death. Then what happens?

Is the energy stored in a carnivore's molecules lost forever when it dies? In the natural world, no potential source of food or energy is wasted. Any time a lion or a great blue heron or any other predator dies, *decomposers* take advantage of the situation. The decaying body of a great blue heron may be gradually broken down by some kinds of bacteria, fungi, and insects.

Decomposers do not just break down the bodies of animals at the top of the food chain. They will consume any form of organic waste—feces, urine, fallen leaves, even the bodies of animals killed by disease. While carnivores may become sick from eating the remains of diseased animals, decomposers can eat just about anything. Even the towering trees of a robust tropical rain forest succumb to such decomposers as pore fungi, amebas, and slime molds.

So far, you have learned about herbivores, carnivores, and decomposers. Every ecosystem also has *omnivores*—animals that eat both plants and other animals. Humans are omnivores, so are the mongooses living on the African plains and the ducks found in almost any small lake in the world. Mongooses eat lizards, snakes, birds, insects, fruits, and berries. Ducks eat insects and a variety of aquatic plants.

Whether they are carnivores or omnivores, whether they live on a grassy savanna or in a small lake, animals living on Earth's surface ultimately depend on plants for food. Without photosynthesis, life as we know it could not exist. Using energy from the Sun, plants manufacture carbohydrates, proteins, and fats. These materials fuel every ecosys-

The Light of Day

tem on Earth. Photosynthesis also produces the oxygen that animals must inhale with every breath.

A CLOSER LOOK AT PHOTOSYNTHESIS

Like all chemical reactions, photosynthesis can be written in the form an equation:

$$6\ CO_2 + 6\ H_2O + light \rightarrow C_6H_{12}O_6 + 6\ O_2.$$

According to this equation, when six molecules of carbon dioxide combine with six molecules of water in the presence of sunlight, the result will be one molecule of glucose and six molecules of oxygen. This seems simple enough, but let's take a closer look.

Each day, solar energy equal to about 1 million exploding atomic bombs reaches Earth's surface. About 1 percent of this energy is captured by plants and used to produce carbohydrates. Solar energy, or *radiation*, comes in many different forms—microwaves, radio waves, gamma rays, X rays, infrared radiation, ultraviolet radiation, and *visible light.*

All types of radiation travel as waves, and waves have different wavelengths. X rays have short wavelengths. Others, such as radio waves, have longer wavelengths. Radiation that travels as shorter waves has more energy than radiation that travels as longer waves. If you look at the *electromagnetic spectrum* on page 15, you will see that waves of ultraviolet radiation are much shorter than radio waves.

You may not realize it, but you are constantly being bombarded by radio waves. It doesn't matter, though. These low-energy rays are completely harmless. If you are exposed to a lot of ultraviolet radiation, however, you will know it because

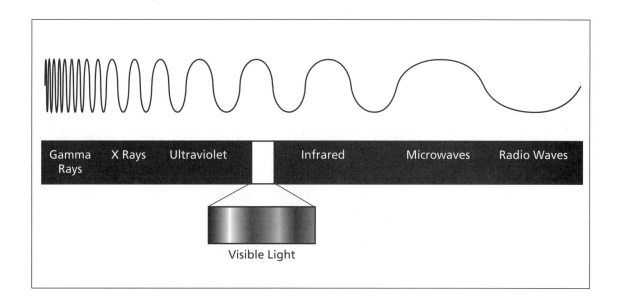

| Gamma Rays | X Rays | Ultraviolet | | Infrared | Microwaves | Radio Waves |

Visible Light

you'll develop a painful sunburn. High-energy radiation can be harmful. That's why people being x-rayed usually wear a heavy lead shield to protect some parts of their bodies.

Near the center of the electromagnetic spectrum is a region called visible light. This is the only type of radiation that we can see. The visible white light emitted by the Sun can be separated into all the colors of the rainbow—red, orange, yellow, green, blue, indigo, and violet. When white light strikes falling raindrops, the water molecules separate the light into these colors and reflect them back toward us. We see a rainbow.

When visible white light strikes any surface on Earth, some of the colors that make up white light are absorbed and others are reflected. We see an object as the color of the light it reflects. For example, the sky looks blue to us because molecules in the air absorb all the colors of visible light except blue. This blue light is reflected and strikes our eyes when we look at the sky.

The electromagnetic spectrum is made of many types of radiation. Each type of radiation has a different wavelength. Only a small portion of the electromagnetic spectrum is visible to us.

When visible white light from the Sun strikes the surface of a leaf, a pigment called *chlorophyll* absorbs the light near the red and blue ends of the visible spectrum. The green light near the center of the spectrum is reflected. That's why most leaves look green to us.

Chlorophyll molecules are located in *chloroplasts*, tiny structures found inside plant cells. In a series of complicated steps, the light energy that chlorophyll absorbs is used to drive a chemical reaction that splits molecules of water, H_2O, into molecules of hydrogen, H_2, and molecules of oxygen, O_2.

$$2\ H_2O \rightarrow 2\ H_2 + O_2$$

The hydrogen molecules, H_2, then combine with carbon dioxide molecules, CO_2, from the air to form glucose, $C_6H_{12}O_6$. The oxygen molecules liberated from water escape from the leaf through pores called stomata. When you walk through a garden on a sunny day, you inhale oxygen given off by the plants around you.

Although scientists began to study the chemical activities of plants more than 350 years ago, it was not until the late 1930s that they understood most of the complex steps of photosynthesis. It did not take this long, however, for scientists to realize the importance of the process.

They knew that Earth's diverse array of life could not have evolved without photosynthesis. Green plants, algae, and cyanobacteria are at the base of the food chain in every ecosystem the scientists knew about—forests, grasslands, deserts, tundra, even coral reefs. These photoautotrophs captured the Sun's energy and used it to convert carbon dioxide and water into the materials that ultimately provide energy to every organism in the ecosystems they had studied. As far as they were concerned, life could not exist without light from the Sun.

CHAPTER TWO

Life in the Deep Sea

We find only the world we look for.

Henry David Thoreau

Around the same time that botanists—scientists who study plants—were working out the intricacies of photosynthesis, a naturalist named William Beebe and an engineer named Otis Barton were about to make a very different type of discovery. In 1934, they became the first people to visit the floor of the deep ocean. Their 4,500-pound (2,040 kg) steel bathysphere with three tiny portholes was lowered to the bottom of the ocean off the coast of Bermuda.

Very few people were interested in this undersea voyage. In the early 1800s, scientists had convinced themselves that the deep sea was not worth exploring. They thought that no life could exist below 2,000 feet (600 m). It was too dark, too cold, and the water pressure was too great.

This view was first challenged in 1860, when a damaged telegraph cable was raised from the deep sea for repairs. The cable was encrusted with living corals, mollusks, and worms. While a few scientists wondered how this was possible, most chose to ignore the evidence before them.

In 1872, the HMS *Challenger* embarked on the first global oceanographic voyage in history. The instructions given to the ship's captain stated, "you have been abundantly supplied with all the instruments and apparatus which modern science and practical experience have been able to suggest and devise....you have a wide field and virgin ground before you."[1]

The scientists onboard used nets, dredges, water samplers, and other equipment lowered from the ship's deck to make measurements and gather samples. This method of compiling data was haphazard at best. Although the scientists did collect a number of deep-sea and bottom-dwelling creatures during the ship's 4-year voyage, once again, these organisms received little attention from the scientific community. The ocean's depths remained then—and remain today—the largest and least-explored wilderness on our planet.

LOOKING BELOW THE SURFACE

As Beebe and Barton, the first people to travel to the ocean floor, prepared for their journey, they could only imagine what they might find 3,038 feet (926 m) below the water's surface. Even they believed that they would probably see very few signs of life. The experience turned out to be a life-altering adventure for both men. In his book, *Half Mile Down*, Beebe wrote:

If one dives and returns to the surface inarticulate with amazement and with a deep realization of the marvel of what he has seen and where he has been, then he deserves to go again and again. If he is unmoved or disappointed, then there remains for him on earth only a longer or shorter period of waiting for death.[2]

William Beebe sits atop the bathysphere that carried him and Otis Barton to the ocean floor.

Life in the Deep Sea

The next major event in deep-sea exploration came in 1960. Swiss engineer Jacques Piccard and United States Navy Lieutenant Don Walsh descended 35,800 feet (10,900 m) to the deepest part of the Pacific Ocean—the Challenger Deep of the Mariana Trench. Their vessel, the *Trieste*, was a bathyscaphe. Piccard described his amazing journey as follows:

> **Like a free balloon on a windless day, indifferent to the almost 200,000 tons of water pressing on the cabin from all sides... slowly, surely, in the name of science and humanity, the *Trieste* took possession of the abyss, the last extreme on our earth that remained to be conquered.[3]**

What have Beebe, Barton, Piccard, Walsh, and the scores of scientists who have followed in their footsteps seen deep below the ocean's surface? Life. And plenty of it—slugs, snails, crabs, bristle worms, ribbon worms, sea anemones, brittle stars, sea cucumbers, fish, octopuses, and many creatures previously unknown to science. Many of these creatures are bizarre-looking relatives of more familiar *species*. Others are more closely related to the fossil remains of long-extinct creatures.

For the last three decades, scientists have been able to explore the ocean depths with submersible vessels like *Alvin*, which is owned by the United States Navy and operated by Woods Hole Oceanographic Institution in Cape Cod, Massachusetts. *Alvin* is a free-roaming vehicle with a telephone-like link to its mother ship. The mother ship—which acts as a floating dormitory, cafeteria, and laboratory for scientists as well as a service garage and launchpad for *Alvin*—gently rolls along the ocean's surface while the submersible plunges into the depths.

On most dives, *Alvin's* passenger compartment transports three adventurous souls—one pilot and two observers—into an unfamiliar world. Since this spherical compartment is only 7 feet (2.1 m) in diameter, the three occupants are squeezed into very cramped quarters. *Alvin's* two mechanical arms, which are operated by the pilot, can collect samples of seawater, rocks, and a variety of living organisms. The submersible is made of titanium, one of the strongest metals on Earth. This tough material must stand up to the tremendous pressure below the ocean's surface. Without it, the crew inside *Alvin* would be crushed.

The bathyscaphe *Trieste* was the first vessel to descend to the deepest part of the ocean.

Alvin sinks at a rate of 100 feet (30 m) per minute and can descend to a maximum depth of 14,700 feet (4,500 m). A typical dive is about 11,000 feet (3,350 m). At such depths, even the strong lights on the submersible do not penetrate far into the blackness.

Life in the Deep Sea

Alvin descends into the depths.

While submersible voyages, as well as investigations performed by unmanned vehicles, have gathered reams of data and collected thousands and thousands of new animal species, less than 5 percent of the ocean floor has been thoroughly explored. In fact, we know more about the landscape of the dark side of the Moon than we do about the landscape of the ocean floor.

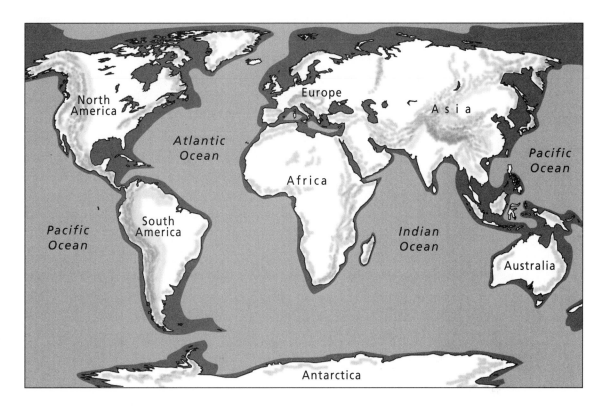

The map shows continents labeled: North America, Europe, Asia, Africa, South America, Australia, Antarctica, and oceans labeled Atlantic Ocean, Pacific Ocean, Indian Ocean.

Scientists know far more about the shallow regions of the ocean called the continental shelves. (The world's continental shelves are shown in dark gray in the diagram above.) The water in these areas, however, accounts for only a fraction of all ocean water. The ecosystems that thrive in these regions of the ocean—intertidal zones and coral reefs—have been well studied. Indeed, many of the fascinating creatures living in these biocommunities can be viewed by any vacationer who completes a short course in scuba diving.

World-renowned oceanographer Jacques-Yves Cousteau developed one of the first underwater breathing devices in the early 1940s. The aqualung allowed divers to remain underwater for hours at a time. Scuba diving has been growing in popularity ever since.

While scientists have learned a great deal about the organisms along the continental shelves (dark gray areas), they know much less about deep-sea ecosystems.

Scuba gear makes it possible for humans to study the diverse array of flora and fauna found in shallow ocean waters. The water there is fairly warm and well lit by the Sun. The pressure is not much of a problem as long as divers do not resurface too quickly.

Scuba diving to the depths of the ocean is impossible, however. The water is icy cold. In the Atlantic, Pacific, and Indian Oceans, water below 325 feet (100 m) is just 36 to 37°F (2 to 3°C). Even if humans could survive such frigid temperatures, there is another, even more serious, problem—water pressure. At a depth of 12,000 feet (3,650 m), the pressure is about 5,000 pounds per square inch (350 kg/cm²). That's like having a small hippopotamus stand on every square inch of your body or being buried beneath about 4,000 feet (1,220 m) of solid rock.

As divers swim farther and farther downward, all of the weight of the water above them presses against their bodies and against the gases inside their scuba tanks. The tanks used by most scuba divers contain the same mixture of gases as normal air—about 78 percent nitrogen, 20 percent oxygen, and 2 percent other compounds.

As divers descend and water pressure increases, the gases in the divers' tanks enter their bloodstreams more quickly. If a diver goes deep enough, the rapid influx of nitrogen into the brain may cause disorientation and loss of coordination. A dive of more than 100 feet (30 m) is extremely dangerous because the divers may lose their sense of direction and have difficulty returning to the surface. They may also forget the importance of returning to the surface slowly and develop a condition called decompression sickness or "the bends." Decompression sickness can cause severe pain, breathing difficulties, and paralysis. In some cases, it can be fatal. As you can see, the ocean's physical properties make deep-sea exploration difficult. Without submersibles and robotic vehicles, it would be impossible.

ADAPTING TO THE DEEP SEA

It's not surprising that scientists in the early 1800s were convinced that the deep sea was devoid of life. They could not imagine organisms that could tolerate the icy cold waters, the tremendous pressure, and the absence of light. At that time, scientists still knew very little about *terrestrial* creatures and the history of life on Earth. They did not appreciate the amazing traits and behaviors some living things have developed to survive in environments that we consider severe. In short, they greatly underestimated life's ability to adapt in order to meet the demands of even the harshest habitats.

An appreciation for what evolution can accomplish has gradually grown during the twentieth century as scientists have studied the farthest reaches of our planet—tropical rain forests, hot springs, Antarctica, and the deepest regions of the ocean.

As *Alvin* begins a typical dive, the ocean's water is clear and visibility is good. The crew sees mats of photosynthetic phytoplankton, large schools of fish, and, perhaps, an occasional shark swimming in the distance.

Soon, the water grows deep blue. Below 450 feet (137 m), there is no longer enough sunlight to power photosynthesis. As *Alvin* continues its downward journey, the water becomes still darker until the vessel is shrouded in complete darkness. Or is it?

Believe it or not, scientists looking out *Alvin's* viewports see something that resembles a star-filled sky. They are not looking at suns millions of miles away; they are seeing an assortment of glowing creatures just a few yards away.

Some of these small light-producing, or *bioluminescent*, animals look like something out of a horror movie. They have huge eyes that are supersensitive to light and massive jaws and teeth. These ferocious deep-sea predators use their lights to lure prey.

The female anglerfish has a fishing rod-like filament protruding from its head. The bait is a glowing bulb. As the fish swims, the bulb waves back and forth, attracting curious prey. Before the helpless victim realizes the peril it's in, the anglerfish devours it. The fish's light allows it to save energy because it does not have to hunt—food comes to it.

The anglerfish uses a glowing tip of flesh to lure prey within range of its razor-sharp teeth.

The hatchetfish has small, needle-sharp teeth that fill its huge, gaping mouth. The fish's lower jaw can open wide enough to snap up a catch as large as it is. Bulbous eyes swell from its narrow head, and a row of bioluminescent organs light up the bottom half of its body. These lights confuse enemies swimming below it. When a predator looks up at a hatchetfish, it is temporarily blinded by sudden flashes of light.

Sloane's viper fish is another bioluminescent deep-sea predator. It has a mouth full of razor-sharp teeth and light-producing organs, called photophores, on its belly.

A variety of other creatures—worms, shrimp, snails, clams, squids, octopuses, fish, corals, bacteria—use their lights to attract mates, confuse predators, or communicate with one another.

Even in the dark depths of the deep ocean, flashlight fish—also called lantern-eye fish—can be seen from 100 feet (30 m) away. They use the light organs under each eye to find food and communicate with other flashlight fish. Flashlight fish can cover their light-producing organs with a screen of dark tissue called a *melanophore.* In this way, they can turn their light on and off, just like you can turn a flashlight on and off.

The flashlight fish's light organs consist of a series of tubes that are teeming with bacteria—one drop of the fluid from these tubes contains about 500,000 bacteria. It is the bacteria that produce the light. The bacteria and the fish have a *symbiotic* relationship. The word "symbiosis" has Greek origins; the first part—sym—means "together," and the second part—bios—means "life." A scientists named Anton deBary coined the term in 1876 to describe organisms of different species that live together.

In the case of flashlight fish and bioluminescent bacteria, both organisms benefit because each one performs a service for the other. The bacteria light up the fish's world, and the fish provides the bacteria with all the food they need. The fish delivers nutrients to the bacteria via blood vessels that run through the tubes where the bacteria live. Mutualism makes life easier for both organisms.

One-quarter of all squids are bioluminescent. Different species of squid produce their bioluminescence in different ways. Like Sloane's viper fish, some deep-sea squids manufacture their light themselves in photophores. Others produce a substance that they store until they feel threatened. When a predator draws too near, the squid secretes the substance into the water. As soon as the substance mixes with oxygen in the water, it glows and distracts the squid's enemy. The predator's confusion gives the squid time to escape. Still other squids have a symbiotic relationship with bioluminescent bacteria, just like flashlight fish.

A bioluminescent squid

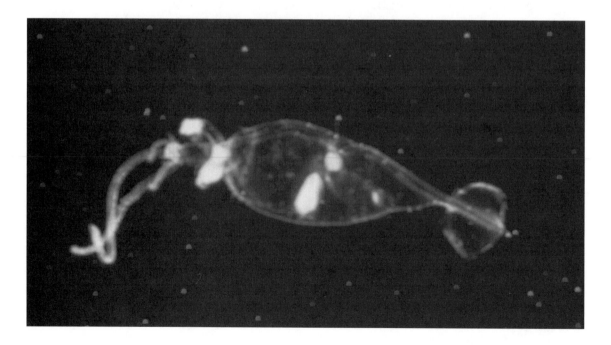

Bioluminescence is just one of the special traits deep-sea animals have developed to survive in their demanding environment. They must also have ways to deal with the incredible pressure and chilly temperatures of the deep sea. For the most part, these animals have learned to go with the flow.

They have fluid-filled, jellyfish-like sacs inside their bodies. The pressure of the fluid in these sacs increases and decreases to match the pressure of the surrounding water. Deep-sea animals are also more *buoyant* than their relatives in the shallow regions of the ocean because they have weaker skeletons and are less muscular. They can get away with these adaptations because they do not have to struggle against tossing waves or powerful undertow.

The white, trumpet-shaped body of a glass sponge seems as delicate as an antique crystal vase. From the sponge's skeleton protrude a number of complex, interlaced stalks that look like fine hairs of spun glass. A variety of small sea stars, sea anemones, and other *invertebrates* are often attached to these stalks.

The giant barrel sponge, which may grow to 6 feet (2 m) in height, looks like a huge vat with evenly spaced vertical ridges along its body. This sponge and the orange and white rope sponge seem just as flimsy as their glassy relatives. The beauty of these elegant creatures can only be appreciated in their underwater environment. Lifting them to the surface tears their delicate bodies to shreds.

These sponges and all other deep-sea creatures are able to survive the cold water of their habitat because their body temperature changes to match the temperature of the water around them.

Being *cold-blooded* is not so uncommon. Many terrestrial creatures—turtles, snakes, frogs, insects, salamanders—and most shallow-ocean inhabitants are cold-blooded, too. Have you ever seen a snake curled up on a dark rock on a warm, sunny summer morning? The snake was trying to warm up because when it's body temperature is higher, it can move more quickly. A fast, nimble snake has a much better chance of catching a mouse than a slow, lethargic snake.

Deep-sea predators never see the light of day, so they can never use the Sun's rays to warm up. As a result, most move rather slowly. Fortunately for them, their prey—which is also cold-blooded—can't warm up either. In fact, deep-sea animals may consume energy at rates ten times lower than the shallow-ocean dwellers that bask in the Sun's rays all day long.

It's a good thing that deep-ocean creatures don't have to use a lot of energy trying to stay warm. As you now know, before an organism can expend energy, it must obtain energy from the food it eats. And food is scarce at the bottom of the ocean.

There is no light there. Without light, there is no photosynthesis. If there is no photosynthesis, there can be no plants. On land, plants are at the base of nearly every food chain. So what do creatures in the deep sea eat?

Most feed on tiny specks of waste that have drifted down from the upper regions of the ocean. This *marine snow* perpetually showers down toward the seafloor. It consists of hundreds of tiny skeletons held together by a mucuslike substance derived from the creatures that originally ate them. At least 30 percent of the material that covers the surface of the ocean floor is marine snow.

Most of the skeletons that make up marine snow come from animals that live in coral reefs or intertidal zones. Marine snow can also contain phytoplankton and algae, which spend the whole day absorbing sunlight and conducting photosynthesis. Because these tiny organisms depend on the Sun, so do the deep-sea animals that eat them. Even though the bizarre creatures in the depths of the ocean never see the shining Sun, they depend on its rays for survival. The Sun ultimately supplies the food they eat as well as the oxygen they breathe.

Particles of marine snow may be recycled many times on their way to the bottom as the waste products of one animal are ingested by another. Each time marine snow is consumed, more of its nutritional value is lost. By the time the particles reach the ocean floor, they contain few of the materials deep-sea creatures need to grow and reproduce. Bottom-feeders must filter the seafloor ooze for hours at a time just to gather enough of these materials to live.

Herds of nearly transparent sea cucumbers crawl across the ocean floor. As they go, they vacuum up the marine snow, remove the nutrients they can use, and leave behind a meandering trail of waste. Some use tentacles to stuff the sediment into their mouths.

THE DIVERSITY OF DEEP-OCEAN LIFE

As scientists explore the ocean floor, they see hundreds of tracks crisscrossing the sediment. Some have been made by recognizable animals, such as sea cucumbers, and some have been made by creatures that no human has yet seen. While scientists have collected and named hundreds of thousands of deep-sea organisms, there are still many more they know nothing about.

Some scientists believe that there may be as many as 100 million species inhabiting the ocean depths. This range of species is greater than that of any terrestrial ecosystem—including tropical rain forests.[4] On one expedition, Fred

Grassle, Director of Marine and Coastal Sciences at Rutgers University in New Brunswick, New Jersey, collected 800 completely new species of organisms in an area about the size of a classroom.

There are the deep-sea sea stars that scurry along the ocean floor at a speed of 24 inches (61 cm) per minute; creamy yellow sea pens that drift along with their frilly plumes oriented into the current so they can snatch passing debris; and comb jellies with rows of sparkling comblike plates that line their translucent pink bodies.

There are sea squirts that spin butterfly-shaped webs of mucus around their 3-inch-long (7.5-cm) bodies to trap marine snow; siphonophores living in bead necklace-shaped colonies lined with stinging cells that may be more than 60 feet (18 m) long; and flowerlike sea lilies that dine on drifting marine snow.

These are just a few of the amazing animals that roam the dark, frigid depths of Earth's oceans. Their bizarre physical characteristics seem well worth scientists' attention. In the future, they may provide valuable information about the evolution of life on Earth. The unusual chemicals in their bodies may even be used to improve industrial processes, break down toxic wastes, or offer potential cures for a host of human ailments.

While the prospect of discovering new, fascinating creatures was the main objective of early deep-sea oceanographers, scientists now know that the deep sea has much more to offer. As you will learn in Chapter 3, the floor of the deep ocean holds the answer to a question that puzzled geologists for decades.

High above the ocean floor, *Alvin* hangs suspended from its mother ship.

This computer generated map shows the location of Earth's mountains and ocean ridges. The Mid-Atlantic Ridge is the light blue line between the Americas and Europe/Africa.

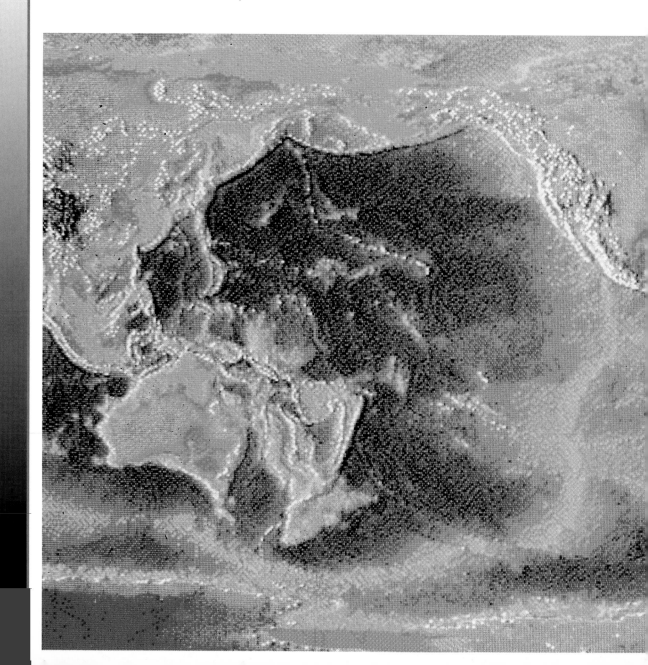

This bioluminescent fish is ready to take a chunk out of any unsuspecting prey that passes by.

A bioluminescent comb jelly

A flashlight fish can turn its light on and off by covering its light-producing organs.

A cluster of deep-sea anemones

Scalding hot water billows from a group of rock chimneys at a site scientists have names Smoke and Mirrors. Hydrothermal vents are home to an amazing assortment of creatures, such as red-tipped tubeworms.

These twin deep-sea chimneys are spouting hot water full of inky sulfides.

Giant, chocolate-brown mussels and pale-white crabs can be found living near some hydrothermal vents.

These creatures live close to a vent near the Galapagos Islands.

CHAPTER THREE

More Treasures from the Deep Sea

Things fall apart; the centre cannot hold;
Mere anarchy is loosed upon the world...

W. B. Yeats, *The Second Coming*

Not all of the scientists exploring the ocean's depths are interested in its odd assortment of organisms. While biologists concentrate on understanding the physical traits and behavioral patterns of deep-sea creatures, geologists focus their attention on the massive underwater mountain ranges that circle Earth's surface like the stitching on a baseball.

These mighty rock formations are called *midocean ridges.* They bisect the Atlantic Ocean; extend through the Indian Ocean; continue around Antarctica; and slice the Pacific Ocean from north to south—temporarily moving onto land as the San Andreas Fault in California and then returning to the ocean off the coast of Washington State.

The tale the ocean ridges have to tell has been pieced together by scientists over the last several decades. In 1912, German meteorologist Alfred Wegener proposed the theory of *continental drift*. According to Wegener, continents and oceans had changed positions over time. In fact, if you look at a map, you can see that the shapes of the continents seem to fit together like the pieces of a jigsaw puzzle. If South America were tipped slightly, its eastern coast would complement the western coast of Africa. If Madagascar were shifted north slightly, it could nestle between eastern Africa and India. Antarctica could fit nicely below India.

Dr. Alfred Wegener was the first scientist to propose that continents move.

Fossil evidence seemed to support Wegener's idea. The fossil remains of tropical plants had been discovered in some parts of North America. Apparently, parts of this continent were once as warm as Ecuador, Brazil, and Columbia are today.

In addition, rock deposits from glaciers had been found in Australia, South America, and Africa. This suggested that, at one time, the climate on these continents was much colder. Perhaps they were located closer to the South Pole at some point in Earth's history.

Had land masses moved over time? Scientists all over the world wondered. They could not imagine the continents, which are now separated by vast oceans, joined together into a single supercontinent. Even Wegener could not explain what geological mechanisms might have been responsible for the movement. Because no one could provide a solution to this critical question, most scientists rejected Wegener's idea.

Not until several years after scientists finished mapping the midocean ridges did all the pieces of the puzzle begin to fall into place. By that time, geologists knew that Earth consists of four layers. The continents and the ocean floor are part of the outermost layer, called the *crust*. The crust is by

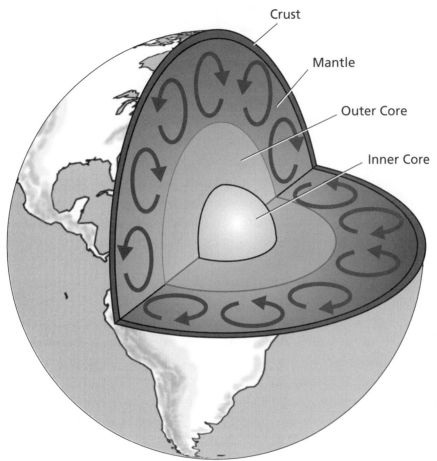

Crust

Mantle

Outer Core

Inner Core

Scientists have divided Earth's interior into four layers: the inner core, the outer core, the mantle, and the crust. Each region has unique physical charateristics.

far the thinnest of the layers. If Earth were an orange, the crust would be thinner than the rind.

Beneath the crust is a 1,800-mile (2,900-km)-thick layer of hot rock called the *mantle*. Below the mantle is Earth's *core* region. The 1,400-mile (2,250-km)-thick outer core layer is composed of liquid iron and nickel. Inside this is the inner layer of the core, which is a little larger than the Moon and made of solid iron and nickel.

More Treasures from the Deep Sea

The innermost regions of the mantle may reach temperatures of 7,500°F (4,150°C). Most of this heat is generated by an internal process called *radioactive decay.* Unlike the core, which is made almost entirely of iron and nickel, the mantle contains large quantities of silicon dioxide, or *silica.*

It also contains chemically unstable forms of *elements* like potassium, uranium, thorium, and carbon. The only way that the atoms of these elements can become more stable is by giving up some of their material. Radioactive decay, the chemical reaction that releases this material, frees a tiny bit of heat energy from the elements.

Because these reactions are happening all the time and because some atoms must go through a number of reactions to become stable, the total amount of heat produced by radioactive decay is enormous. As it turns out, this vast reservoir of heat drives a complex process that does exactly what Wegener proposed. It causes the continents to slowly drift.

Because the rock in the mantle is so hot, it is softer than rocks on Earth's surface. Rock in Earth's mantle has the consistency of stiff oatmeal and can be squeezed this way and that like toothpaste inside a partially used tube with the cap on.

Hot rock in the deepest layers of the mantle pushes upward toward the cooler crust. When the rock reaches the mantle-crust border, it travels along the border and releases heat to the crust. When the mantle rock is cooler than the rock below it, it is forced downward. The rock returns to the deepest regions of the mantle where it is reheated, continuing the cycle.

This type of movement, called *convection,* can be observed in any fluid. When a covered pot of water is heated on the

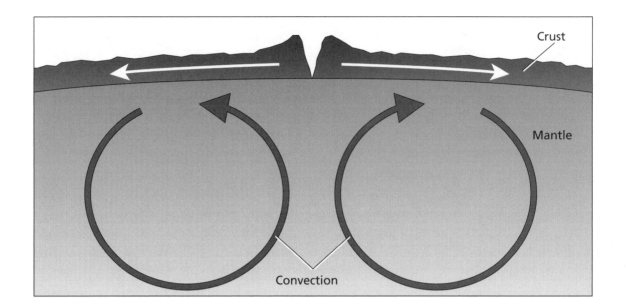

Crust

Mantle

Convection

stove, the water closest to the burner heats up and moves toward the top of the pot. When the heated water rises, it is replaced by cooler water from above. Over time, a cycle or current is created within the pot. This convection current continues until the water is transformed to a gas—steam—or the burner is turned off.

The mantle's molten magma is never heated so much that it escapes as a gas, and its heat source, radioactive decay, is never turned off. It has been churning the mantle's rock for more than 4 billion years. The mantle is so thick and the movement so gradual, that it may take hundreds of millions of years to complete a single loop. When heat from deep within Earth's interior reaches the surface of the crust, it is released through volcanoes, *geysers,* and *hydrothermal vents.* A volcano erupts occasionally, spewing lava that destroys everything in its path. Geyers and hydrothermal vents spout superheated water that has been exposed to the tremendous heat and pressure below Earth's surface.

Convection currents in the Earth's mantle cause some parts of the crust to tear. The result can be a large trench, such as the one at the center of the Mid-Atlantic Ridge.

Hot Springs and Hydrothermal Vents

When the heat from deep within Earth's interior reaches the crust, it is released through tears in Earth's surface. In some cases, the fracture extends all the way through the crust and molten magma periodically erupts through the vents as lava. When this lava cools, it forms a mountain called a volcano.

In other cases, the fracture is not complete, so magma cannot escape. However, heat from the mantle's molten magma is absorbed by the solid rocks at the base of the crust. This heat is then transferred to water that has seeped into the fracture.

When a tear occurs along the ocean floor, the seawater that enters the hole is superheated until it becomes more buoyant than the ocean water above it. Then the seawater spews back into the ocean with a force similar to that of water gushing from an open fire hydrant. The hydrothermal vent releases fluid until changes in the area's geology block the vent.

Sometimes, Earth's internal heat escapes through a geyser on land. A geyser is one type of natural *hot spring*. It is different from other hot springs because it occasionally roars to life and blasts a mixture of steam and water hundreds of feet into the air. The water that fuels a geyser comes from a network of natural tubes and caverns below the geyser's vent. This water is heated by the same layer of rock as the seawater that gushes from hydrothermal vents.

There are about 800 geysers in the world. More than half are located in Yellowstone National Park in the United States. Earth's three other major geyser fields are in Russia, New Zealand, and Iceland. You should not be surprised to hear that one geyser field is in Iceland. If you look at the map on page 41, you'll see that Iceland is very close to the Mid-Atlantic Ridge.

Even though a geyser and a hydrothermal vent form in exactly the same way, they release material differently. If a geyser periodically erupts with bursts of steam and water, why does a hydrothermal vent release a steady, continuous billow of mineral-laden fluid? The answer can be found by considering another question: What is the difference between a terrestrial environment and a deep-ocean environment? The answer is obvious—water.

The ocean contains millions and millions of gallons of water, so there is always plenty of water to replace the water that is spewing from a hydrothermal vent. A geyser erupts periodically because it has no constant water source. When a geyser gushes, all of the water in its underground network is lost. The geyser cannot erupt again until water from rain and melted snow refills its network of tubes and caverns. This process can take a few minutes, a few hours, or a few days.

Water is much heavier than air. The water at the bottom of the ocean is under a lot of pressure because it bears the weight of all the water above it. As pressure increases, the temperature at which a liquid transforms into a gas, such as steam, also increases. A geyser releases a combination of steam and water because some of the superheated water boils and becomes a gas. Even though the material spewed by hydrothermal vents is just as hot, the tremendous pressure at the bottom of the ocean prevents the seawater from transforming into steam.

Geysers like this one are a common site at Yellowstone National Park.

The first hydrothermal vent was discovered in 1977 along a portion of midocean ridge called the Galapagos Rift, which takes its name from the nearby Galapagos Islands in the Pacific Ocean. When more hydrothermal vents were found along the Mid-Atlantic Ridge, the portion of midocean ridge that runs through the center of the Atlantic Ocean, scientists realized that there must be a connection between underwater mountain formation and these vents. Working out this connection required examining data from a variety of sources and integrating a number of different theories that had been proposed during the 1950s and 1960s.

Scientists believe that Earth's relatively thin crust is broken into slabs of rock, called *plates.* There are six very large plates and about a dozen smaller ones. Wherever the edges of two plates meet, the mantle's convection currents cause the plates to either push against each other or pull apart from one another.

If convection currents are pushing the plates together, *subduction* occurs. This means that one of the colliding plates rides up over the other one. For example, the southern part of the American Plate moves over the Nazca Plate and pushes the edge of the Nazca Plate down into the hot mantle rock, melting it. Wherever subduction occurs, continents are slowly drifting closer together.

In other parts of the world, convection currents are causing plates to move farther away from each other. This process, called *seafloor spreading,* is happening along the Mid-Atlantic Ridge. Because the floor of the Atlantic Ocean is spreading, the United States and Europe are currently being pulled apart at a rate of about 1 inch (2.5 cm) each year. Your fingernails grow at about the same rate.

As the northern part of the American Plate moves away from the Eurasian Plate and the southern part of the American Plate moves away from the African Plate, the fracture between them grows larger and larger. Occasionally, lava erupts from the fracture. When the lava comes into contact with the frigid waters of the deep Atlantic, it hardens and forms new ocean floor. This is how midocean ridges are built. At the center of the Mid-Atlantic Ridge is a 0.6-mile (1-km)-wide *rift valley*—a deep trench along the top of the ridge. This massive valley is much deeper than the Grand Canyon.

At some locations along the rift valley, seawater seeps down into the sizzling-hot crust and upper mantle. As the water moves downward, it is heated to temperatures as high as 750°F (400°C). Even though freshwater normally boils at

Because the Nazca Plate and the southern part of the American Plate are pushing against one another, the Nazca Plate is pushed down into the hot mantle and melts.

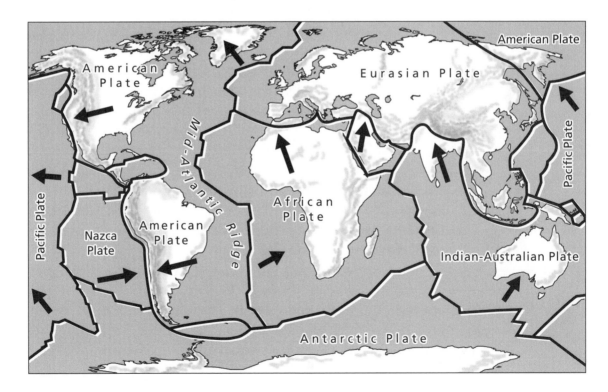

More Treasures from the Deep Sea

212°F (100°C) and transforms into steam, this seawater is under so much pressure that it does not become a gas. At a pressure of 250 atmospheres, which is equal to 4,000 pounds per square inch (280 kg/cm^2), seawater will not boil until it reaches 730°F (390°C).

A rich assortment of precious and semiprecious metals—iron, copper, silver, zinc, tin, cobalt, and lead—in the rock below Earth's surface dissolve in the water as it grows hotter and hotter. Sulfate, a substance common in deep-sea water, is converted to hydrogen sulfide, which has the unpleasant odor of rotten eggs.

Because the mineral-rich, superheated liquid is more buoyant than the cooler water above, it pushes upward toward the ocean floor. It moves through the fractured crust and reemerges through the hydrothermal vents along the rift valley. Sometimes the liquid flows out of a vent as a gentle trickle. In other cases, it blasts ferociously into the frigid ocean. The fluid may spout up to 650 feet (200 m) above the seafloor before it blends in with the surrounding water.

As soon as the superheated solution mixes with the 36°F (2°C) water of the deep ocean, the materials dissolved in it separate from the solution and become visible particles. The result is a hot black or white "smoke" of minerals. Like the lava that flows out of a volcano, the minerals that spew out of a hydrothermal vent are deposited around its edges. In the case of a volcano, the built-up lava forms a mountain. In the case of a hydrothermal vent, the built up minerals form colorful undersea "chimneys."

These mineral chimneys come in a variety of sizes, shapes, and colors. Some are stout. Others are tall and slim. Still others have onion-shaped domes. They may be orange, green, brown, or white, depending on the kinds of minerals they contain. The minerals that pour out of the hottest vents form dark chimneys called *black smokers*.

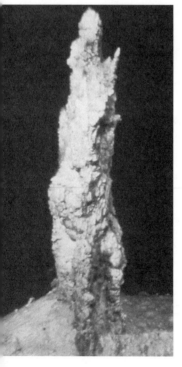

Deep-sea chimneys like this one are formed by minerals in the water that spews from hydrothermal vents.

In some cases, the shapes of mineral chimneys have captured the imagination of the scientists who discovered them. These chimneys bear names like Statue of Liberty, Eiffel Tower, Kremlin, Beehive, the Alps, and Wasps' Nest. An enormous black smoker along the Juan de Fuca Ridge in the Pacific Ocean was appropriately dubbed Godzilla. This chimney was once taller than a thirteen-story building and more than 40 feet (12 m) in diameter.

CHIMNEYS ARE JUST THE BEGINNING

These breathtaking mineral chimneys are not the only treasures discovered by the scientists who have explored hydrothermal vents. At some sites, they have encountered long, white spaghetti-like worms draped in stringy bundles over mounds of black basalt. Close by, clumps of Jericho tubeworms twist about each other like snakes, evoking images of Medusa's head.[1] Meanwhile, miniature lobsters move among clusters of giant clams in search of a meal and swarms of porcelain-white shrimp crawl over the surface of black smokers.[2]

The unusual biological communities that grow up around hydrothermal vents continue to surprise and delight scientists. "Few discoveries in science come completely unexpected," says Holger Jannasch, a microbiologist at Woods Hole Oceanographic Institution. "This is one of them."[3] By 1977, scientists believed they had a basic understanding of how all the world's ecosystems work. Vent communities challenged their theories.

As you will learn in the next chapter, vent organisms are startlingly different from their deep-sea neighbors. Perhaps the most important difference is the types of food they eat. The creatures living in the water surrounding hydrothermal vents do not rely on the marine snow that cascades down from the upper regions of the ocean. Vent communities generate their own food. Plants are not at the base of this ecosystem's food chain, bacteria are. Energy does not come from the Sun's rays; it comes from hydrogen sulfide, the smelly compound that spews out of the ocean floor. Vent communities do not fit the ecosystem model that had been carefully developed by scientists who had studied terrestrial and shallow-ocean ecosystems for decades.

Vent organisms captured the imaginations of scientists because they were surviving, and thriving, under seemingly impossible conditions. They even challenged the most basic of all biological questions: What is necessary for life? At one time, sunlight had been at the top of the list. Suddenly scientists were faced with an ecosystem where there seemed to be life without light. They had found a place that met two important criteria: a vent community receives no sunlight and its food chain does not depend upon photosynthetic organisms. Instead of photoautotrophs, vent communities depend on *chemoautotrophs*—creatures that get the energy they need from chemicals, such as hydrogen sulfide, and do not rely on other living things for food.

CHAPTER FOUR

Hydrothermal Vent Communities

So many questions, so many mysteries.
It is only by going down ourselves to the depths
of the sea that we can hope to clear them up.

Auguste Piccard

On February 15, 1977, a team of geologists was cruising along the ocean's surface about 650 miles (1,050 km) southwest of Panama and 200 miles (320 km) north of the Galapagos Islands. Deep below the surface, their equipment snapped photographs every 10 seconds and continuously monitored the water temperature. The team's mission was to study the geology and chemistry of the Galapagos Rift.

As scientists onboard the research vessel *Knorr* watched the instruments receiving data from below, they noticed an unusual jump in water temperature. After the equipment was hauled up, the geologists waited impatiently while the film was processed. What the photos revealed—hundreds of clams—surprised them all. There weren't supposed to be clams living on the floor of the deep ocean. This was the first time that any human had caught a glimpse of a hydrothermal vent community.

Lulu, a small catamaran with *Alvin* onboard, arrived at the site the following afternoon. The next morning, the submersible and its three passengers found themselves in a 65-foot (20-m)-wide deep-sea oasis teeming with life. Geologist Jack Corliss sent a simple, awestruck message to the crew onboard the *Knorr*: "There's all these animals down here." He continued:

> **Besides the overlapping huge white clams—some the size and shape of old-fashioned oval china dinner plates at the corner diner—[Corliss] saw skittering white crabs, chunky albino lobsters as big as a boxer's fist, and clusters of bizarre flower-like creatures looking for all the world like overgrown orangish dandelions about to burst with seed. As *Alvin* paused, white crabs clambered into the sub's specimen tray. This was anything but a lifeless desert.[1]**

As the scientists continued to explore the rift, they found dozens of hydrothermal vents and many more vent communities. Because the trip had begun as a search for unusual geological phenomena, there were no biologists onboard the *Knorr*. As the geologists, many of whom hadn't taken a biology class since high school, described the bizarre vent creatures to biologists at Woods Hole Oceanographic Institution via radio transmissions, the life scientists were dumbfounded. Many of the organisms being described were unlike anything they had ever encountered. One crew member described his impressions in a series of letters to his girlfriend, a biologist at Woods Hole:

I have specimens for you…. I do not have a white clam as they have found only one alive…. I have also collected some lobsterlike critters that get into the sub while it's on the bottom…. We could use a biologist down here.

…there are great stringlike networks of worms or something like that. It looks like someone dumped spaghetti all over the lava rocks. I really think the biology story here is as big if not bigger than the geology story…. Boy, I wish you were here….

In all of these oases are the crabs…hopping up onto and into the sub. Now the fish of the area come to these warm vents and sort of lounge around in the warm water. They actually get into the warm water steam and roll over and bask….

All of the life is clustered around the vents. Away from the vents, life is as it usually is at that depth. Kind of boring. The warm areas are very small, 4 to 5 m [13 to 16 feet], but the warming effect seems to reach out to maybe a 10 to 20 m [33 to 66 foot] radius. There seems to be a lot of these vents, but we have only really looked at four of them.[2]

The first scientists to view hydrothermal vents saw all sorts of animal life, including pale-white crabs scavenging for food on bacteria-covered rocks.

Robert Ballard, who is now the director of the Center for Marine Exploration at Woods Hole Oceanographic Institute, was one of the scientists on this amazing voyage of discovery. Even today, he is struck by the fact that the team onboard *Knorr* discovered the first vent community so close to the site where, nearly 100 years earlier, Charles Darwin had furiously scribbled notes about species diversity in the log onboard the HMS *Beagle*.

Years later Darwin would return to these notes and use his observations as evidence for an idea now known as *natural selection*. Darwin's theory changed the way scientists looked at the relationships between living things. It also led scientists to ask questions about the origin of life on Earth. Although Darwin's ideas were not accepted by his contemporaries, scientists have since found a great deal of evidence that supports them.

Today scientists all over the world embrace the basic principles of the theory of natural selection. It is difficult to refute that the species that currently inhabit Earth have evolved from more primitive species that lived millions of years ago.

The discovery of hydrothermal vent communities has also altered scientists' view of the natural world. These vent communities have shown us that our original ecosystem models were not complete. The complex interactions among vent organisms have raised new questions about the origin of life on our planet. You will find out more about this in Chapter 8, but for now, let's return to the midocean ridge.

EXPLORING THE MID-ATLANTIC RIDGE

In 1985, Peter Rona, a marine geologist at Rutgers University in New Brunswick, New Jersey, explored the seafloor of the Atlantic Ocean. He was surprised to discover dozens of black smokers along a portion of the Mid-Atlantic Ridge 1,800

miles (2,900 km) east of Miami, Florida. This was the first hydrothermal vent field discovered in the Atlantic.

As Rona explored the vent community, he observed a variety of astonishing undersea animals, including a type of eyeless shrimp. With the help of Austin Williams, of the Smithsonian Institution in Washington, D.C., Rona found that no one had previously identified this species of shrimp. The two men decided to name the shrimp *Rimicaris exoculata,* which means "dweller in the rift without eyes." Over the next few years, scientists found many more vents and vent communities in the Atlantic Ocean. Even today, new vents are being discovered all the time. Many more remain to be found.

Even for scientists who have spent countless hours wandering along the seafloor in submersible vessels, finding a new vent community recaptures the feelings expressed by Beebe when he returned from the very first dive into the deep ocean.

It is, indeed, the experience of a lifetime. That's because no one knows exactly what he or she will encounter at a new vent site. No two vents are the same. The size, shape, and color of undersea chimneys vary from site to site. The creatures that inhabit the surrounding waters vary, too. While scientists have identified several hundred previously unknown species around vents, the number of different species living around any one vent is usually quite small.

Do Vents Give Off Light?

As one of the first vent organisms identified, rift shrimp have endured more than their share of poking and prodding. Scientists were not too surprised to find that this shrimp has no eyes on its head. Many cave dwellers lack eyes, too. After all, what use are eyes in a pitch-dark environment?

That's why a graduate student's discovery shocked scientists around the world. In 1986, Cindy Lee Van Dover was looking for a research project. Her advisor, Fred Grassle, a researcher at Woods Hole Oceanographic Institute, suggested that she study rift shrimp, which had first been collected by Peter Rona a year earlier.

As Van Dover watched videotapes of the shrimp in their natural environment, she noticed that they had a pair of bright patches on their backs. When the shrimp were brought to the surface, the patches lost their brightness and blended in with the rest of the creature's tough outer shell.

When Van Dover looked closely at her specimens, she could barely see the strange patches. She decided to dissect the patches and see if she could figure out if they served any special purpose. Each patch was attached to a large nerve. The patches seemed to be some type of sense organs. Could they be eyes?

She sent her specimens to Steve Chamberlain, a neuroscientist at Syracuse University in Syracuse, New York, who specializes in invertebrate eyes. Although exposure to bright light had injured the tissue,

The shrimp that Rona encountered in the middle of the Atlantic are very common in vent communities along the Mid-Atlantic Ridge, while giant clams and mussels with golden or chocolate-colored shells are more prevalent in vent ecosystems along the East Pacific Rise. Many vent species appear to be site specific.

Scientists are not sure how the vent organisms found at a number of sites are able to travel through the frigid water

Chamberlain was fairly certain that he was looking at photoreceptors. "I could imagine what it looked like before it got screwed up," he says. "If you destroyed an eye, this is what it would look like."[3]

Now Van Dover had a new question. What was the shrimp looking at? Because the patches have no lenses, the shrimp couldn't form an image. So, in fact, it wasn't looking at anything. But the shrimp was using the photoreceptors to catch photons, rays of light. What could the source of this light be? There only seemed to be one answer—vent light that was outside the range of human vision.

To see if she was right, Van Dover asked John Delaney of the University of Washington in Seattle to film the area surrounding a vent with a sensitive digital video camera. As Van Dover waited impatiently onboard the *Atlantis II*, Delaney descended in *Alvin* to a vent just off the coast of Washington State. A few hours later, Van Dover received a two-word message from the ocean floor: "Vents glow."

No one knows what causes hydrothermal vents to glow or if the shrimp can actually sense the light. But if they can, Van Dover says, "the light could serve as a beacon to draw them to areas where they can feed and such a light could also serve as a warning signal to deter them from too close an encounter with water hot enough to cook them instantly."[4] The significance of vent light will be discussed in greater detail in Chapter 8.

This photo of giant clams was taken at the deep-sea vent named Clam Acres.

of the deep sea to populate new vents. They are also unsure about how these organisms find new vent sites. Do the organisms respond to some sort of chemical pulse generated by the seafloor eruption that creates a new vent or is locating a new vent literally a shot in the dark?

What scientists do know is that only about one-third of vent species have recognizable relatives in the deep ocean. In fact, many appear to be more closely related to species that have long been extinct.

The dominant or most extraordinary member of a particular vent community often determines how scientists name the site. For example, at vent sites named Clam Acres, Clam Bake I, and Mussel Bed the seafloor is carpeted with shellfish the size of footballs. Snake Pit supports a population of striking, white, eel-like fish. Snow Blower is named for the flaky white bacteria that spewed from the vent when it first formed like a 160-foot (50-m)-tall blizzard.

Dandelion Patch features hundreds of peach-colored, Ping-Pong ball-sized animals floating just above the seafloor.

Their delicate bodies resemble dandelions that have just gone to seed. Like their distant relative, the Portuguese man-of-war, these creatures catch passing prey with stinging tentacles that protrude from their body like pins stuck in a pin cushion.

Many vent communities are dominated by dense fields of crimson-topped giant tubeworms. When such spectacular scenery fills the tiny portholes of a submersible vessel, awed scientists may momentarily forget that their job is to be cautious, questioning, impartial observers. As they are captivated by the vent's unique beauty, their playful—or even romantic—sides inspire them to come up with names like Garden of Eden, East of Eden, and Rose Garden.

AT THE BOTTOM OF IT ALL

While it is often the tall, graceful tubeworms, *crustaceans* such as crabs and shrimp, or *bivalves* such as clams and mussels that first catch scientists' attention, none of these remarkable creatures can be credited with making a vent community a special type of ecosystem. To see the most amazing vent organisms, scientists must look much more closely. In fact, they need a microscope and, in some cases, a scalpel. These instruments are necessary to reveal bacteria—the creatures at the bottom of vent community food chains.

Scientists have identified close to 200 different species of bacteria living in the water around some vents. Heat-loving microorganisms, called *archaebacteria,* live on and in mineral chimneys. They need only nitrogen, carbon dioxide, and hydrogen to survive and reproduce. The nitrogen and carbon are readily available in seawater. The hydrogen is obtained from hydrogen sulfide in the seawater or the basalt rock that has spilled from the vent onto the ocean floor. You will learn more about archaebacteria in Chapter 7.

Other types of bacteria spend their time riding the wave of scalding fluid that is spewed from the hydrothermal vent. This is a dangerous lifestyle because the bacteria are exposed to the elements and are easy prey for hungry zooplankton.

To avoid their enemies, many vent bacteria have found a better way of life. They have moved into a well-guarded home. This safe haven is inside the bodies of giant tube-worms and a few other vent animals. Like the bioluminescent bacteria that make many deep-sea creatures glow, vent bacteria have developed symbiotic relationships with the larger animals in their environment.

A vent animal provides its bacterial tenants with a safe place to live and a constant supply of raw materials—chemicals from the seawater. In exchange, the bacteria convert the chemicals provided by their host into carbohydrates that serve as food for the bacteria as well as the animal. Both have better lives when they work together.

Because a large organism has access to much greater quantities of seawater than do free-floating bacteria, residing in a vent animal allows bacteria to withstand fluctuations in the relative concentrations of chemicals more easily than if they were living independently.

If the animal is in an area that lacks the chemicals its bacteria need, it can simply look elsewhere. A tubeworm's plume is mobile and can stretch this way or that until it finds seawater with the perfect mixture of raw materials.

Every mussel has a "foot" that secretes a tough thread. The mussel can anchor this thread to a nearby rock or other surface and then pull itself closer to the object. If the new site does not have the chemical combination the mussel is looking for, it can move again. This form of locomotion may be slow, but it is good enough to hold up the mussel's end of the symbiotic deal.

INSIDE A TUBEWORM

Dense thickets of 8- to 12-foot (2.4-to-3.7 m)-tall tubeworms are the most prominent members of many hydrothermal vent communities. Their red plumes sit atop long white tubes. The water spouting from the vent and gentle ocean currents toss the tubeworm's tips to and fro. The base of a tubeworm may be anchored to another tubeworm, a mineral chimney, or the layer of black basalt that has recently poured forth from Earth's tumultuous interior.

For all their grace and beauty, tubeworms are hardy creatures that manage to survive under conditions similar to those found at a toxic waste site. Their tubes are their first line of defense against their harsh environment and potential predators. When bachyuran crabs nip at a tubeworm's tender plume with their sharp claws, the tubeworm quickly pulls its plume into the safety of its tube. The tubeworm's quick reflexes are just one of its adaptations for life around a hydrothermal vent.

Tubeworms are nothing at all like the earthworms you may have seen in a garden or used as fishing bait. Besides being much larger, they have no eyes, no mouth, and no digestive tract. A tubeworm's plume consists of many layers of thin waferlike tissue and performs the same function as a fish's gills. A fish uses its gills to obtain oxygen from water; a tubeworm's plume takes in oxygen as well as carbon dioxide and hydrogen sulfide.

A *hemoglobin* molecule in the tubeworm's blood attaches to each molecule of water and hydrogen sulfide absorbed by the plume and carries it through a network of channels to the tubeworm's *trophosome*. (The carbon dioxide is dissolved directly into the tubeworm's blood.) In humans, hemoglobin transports the oxygen we have inhaled from our lungs to

The existence of tubeworms was a complete surprise to scientists.

every cell in our bodies through blood vessels. It is hemoglobin that gives our blood and a tubeworm's plume their bright red color.

The trophosome is the organ where a tubeworm's food-producing bacteria live. When raw materials reach the trophosome, it is time for the bacteria to earn their keep. What these bacteria do is really not all that different from what green plants do. As you learned in Chapter 1, during photosynthesis, green plants convert carbon dioxide and water into glucose and oxygen. For this process to occur, plants require energy from the Sun.

At the bottom of the ocean, there is no sunlight, but there is hydrogen sulfide. The hydrogen sulfide in vent fluid exists as *ions*. An ion is an atom or molecule that has an electrical charge because it has gained or lost an *electron*. An ion of hydrogen sulfide, HS^- has lost an electron, so it has a negative charge. When one of these ions combines with two molecules of oxygen, energy is released. The other products of this reaction—a sulfate ion, SO_4^{-2}, and a hydrogen ion, H^+—are expelled by the bacteria and dissolve into the surrounding seawater.

$$HS^- + 2\ O_2 \rightarrow energy + SO_4^{-2} + H^+$$

As long as carbon dioxide is present in the tubeworm's trophosome, the energy released during this reaction powers a complex series of steps that ultimately produces simple carbohydrates, like glucose. This process, called *chemosynthesis*, provides all the materials that the bacteria and their hosts need to live.

THE VENT COMMUNITY FOOD CHAIN

While organisms at the bottom of a vent community food web are very different from those living in more familiar ecosystems, many of the other creatures seem a little less exotic. You already know that tubeworms, clams, and mussels receive some or all of their food from the bacteria living inside them. But what about the porcelain-white bachyuran crabs, the slow-moving hairy snails, and dozens of other vent creatures? While scientists are still trying to work out the details of vent community food chains, they do know that this community's food chain works just like that of any other ecosystem on Earth—the smaller organisms are hunted by the larger ones.

Tiny zooplankton, *amphipods*, and thumb-sized rift shrimp spend their days riding the fluid gushing from the vent. They eat free-living bacteria found in the billowing vent fluid. Some rift shrimp may also obtain nutrients directly from mineral chimneys. Scientists have observed them digging along the surface of black smokers with the scoop-shaped set of claws closest to their mouths.

While mussels and clams receive most of their food from their symbiotic inhabitants, they may supplement their diet by filter-feeding free-living bacteria. A variety of other vent creatures rely on filter feeding for all of their food. They eat zooplankton that has ventured out of the scalding vent fluid. Like their deep-sea neighbors, vent filter-feeders also eat waste material and other detritus.

If a bachyuran crab wants a square meal, it must grab a tubeworm's bright red plume before the soft-bodied worm can escape into its protective tube. Grazing animals such as hairy snails dine on the mats of archaebacteria that carpet mineral chimneys. Hairy snails also obtain some nourishment from the chemosynthetic bacteria that have taken up residence in the snail's gills. Parasitic copepods infest the plumes of tubeworms, the gills of shrimp, and the backs of crabs. One type of parasitic fungus makes its home in the stomachs of squat lobsters.

Occasional deep-sea visitors are among the animals at the top of a hydrothermal vent community's food chain. Predatory fish and octopuses periodically rush into the hot water around the vent for a quick snack. The eelpout, a pink fish with piercing blue eyes, boldly swims into the vent plume and snaps up bacteria. Other deep-sea predators prefer the fleshy plumes of tubeworms. Still others eat crabs, shrimp, or snails.

A quick dash into the scalding water around the vent is worth the risk for deep-sea predators. A vent meal will provide them with far more energy than a deep-sea dinner consisting of creatures that have fed on recycled marine snow.

Bacteria form thick mats that carpet rocks around many deep-sea vents.

While a lack of available energy and frigid waters slows the pace of life in the deep sea, conditions around a vent are quite different. As a result, vent communities are very densely populated. The *biomass* of a vent community is 500 to 1,000 times greater than it is in the surrounding deep sea. In fact, the productivity of a vent community is comparable to that of a coral reef.[5] (Coral reefs and tropical rain forests have traditionally been considered the most diverse and productive ecosystems on Earth.)

It's not just the tempo of life that's accelerated in a vent community. While terrestrial and deep-sea communities have changed relatively little over millions of years, vent communities come and go relatively quickly. That's because the vents

Another Deep-Sea Ecosystem

As you learned in Chapter 3, hydrothermal vents form along the rift valley of midocean ridges. This is where the seafloor grows as continental plates are pulled apart by convection currents that churn deep below Earth's surface.

As some continental plates move away from one another, other plates collide and the edge of one plate forces the edge of the other into Earth's interior, where it melts. At these sites, called subduction zones, a thick fluid containing methane and other materials slowly oozes into the sea. This material is a source of food for chemosynthesizing microbes that power entire ecosystems.

At first glance, these *seep communities* appear to have a lot in common with vent communities. Both are located at the bottom of the ocean; neither relies on photosynthesis for food; both have giant tubeworms. A closer look, however, shows more differences than similarities.

Even though the giant tubeworms collected at seeps and vents might look the same to us, their behaviors and lifestyles are quite different. It is important to remember that the tubeworms are as diverse a group as the vertebrates, which includes whales and mice, guppies and elephants, eagles and alligators.

Because seep communities do not come and go as quickly as vent communities, seep organisms lead much more stable lives. Tubeworms grow much more slowly here—less than 0.4 inch (1 cm) per year. Also, because the water temperature at a seep site is no different from that of surrounding seawater, deep-sea scavengers visit frequently in search of a hardy meal.

are often changed or destroyed by seafloor movements. Data collected at old vent sites suggest that while some vent communities last only 1 or 2 years, most last about 50 years.

Even the adaptations that allow tubeworms and other vent organisms to live in their toxic environment cannot save them from geological changes deep within our planet. These creatures are dependent on the chemical-rich fluid spewing from the hydrothermal vent. If the geological conditions of the area change and the vent becomes inactive, all the creatures living around it must find a new home very quickly or they will die.

Vent organisms are in a race against time. That may be the reason tubeworms are the fastest-growing marine invertebrate. "They live hard, live fast, and die young," jokes Charles Fisher of the Pennsylvania State University in State College.[6] By injecting dye into their plumes, Fisher has shown that, at some sites, tubeworms grow almost 3 feet (1 m) every year.

A ROLE FOR THE SUN?

Unlike the organisms that inhabit the deep sea, hydrothermal vent organisms appear to be more or less self-sufficient. Their ecosystem is energized not by the Sun's rays, but by hydrogen sulfide. The basic materials that fuel the vent community are created by chemoautotrophs during chemosynthesis, not by photoautotrophs during photosynthesis. Besides hydrogen sulfide, chemosynthesis requires only carbon dioxide and oxygen. Both of these gases are readily available in the seawater surrounding the vent.

Before accepting that this ecosystem is completely free of the Sun's influence, think about one question: How do carbon dioxide and oxygen get into seawater? Much of the carbon dioxide in the ocean was produced billions of years ago when Earth formed. At that time, carbon dioxide was also the primary ingredient in Earth's atmosphere. Today, however, it constitutes less than 2 percent of our atmosphere. That's fortunate for humans, and practically every other living thing, because inhaling too much carbon dioxide can kill most creatures in a matter of seconds.

The most common material in the atmosphere today is oxygen. Where does all that oxygen come from? To answer that question, let's take another look at a chemical reaction discussed in Chapter 1.

$$6\,CO_2 + 6\,H_2O + light \rightarrow C_6H_{12}O_6 + 6\,O_2$$

This is the reaction for photosynthesis. The reactants are carbon dioxide, CO_2; water, H_2O; and radiation from sunlight. The products are glucose, $C_6H_{12}O_6$, the simple carbohydrate that provides most ecosystems with energy, and oxygen, O_2. Photosynthesis is the source of the oxygen that dominates Earth's atmosphere. It is also the source of the oxygen in seawater.

Without the Sun's rays to power photosynthesis, the bacteria found floating freely in the vent's billowing plume and inside tubeworms and other vent animals would have no access to oxygen. Without oxygen, these bacteria could not chemosynthesize. As it turns out, in order to find an ecosystem that is truly independent of the Sun, we must leave the ocean and examine a few unusual ecosystems on land.

CHAPTER FIVE

The Wonder of Caves

> They wound this way and that far down into the secret depths of the cave…. In one place they found a spacious cavern, from whose ceiling descended a multitude of shining stalactites of the length and circumference of a man's leg; they walked all about it, wondering and admiring, and presently left it by one of the numerous passages that opened into it.

Mark Twain, *The Adventures of Tom Sawyer*

Skyscrapers—they are, perhaps, our greatest architectural achievement. Before humans discovered the strength of steel girders, they built a variety of shorter, but equally impressive, structures—sprawling mansions, mighty castles, and grand cathedrals. Even earlier, ancient Egyptians built pyramids to house their dead rulers. Half a world away, the Inca, Maya, and Olmec people constructed pyramids to please their gods.

Since the dawn of civilization, humans have been driven by their desire to build the biggest, most magnificent structures imaginable. There was a time, however, when large groups of people did not live together in one spot. There were no nations with governments; there weren't even cities or towns. People spent their whole lives traveling from place to place in search of food. They hunted animals and gathered leaves, fruits, and roots. These people lived in small, temporary shelters such as huts made of grass, mud, and tree bark or tents made of animal skins. When the food supply began to dwindle in one area, they moved to another.

And even before that, our ancestors lived in caves. As they explored the underground caverns and passages, they were no doubt amazed by what they saw—huge *stalactites* hanging down from the caves' ceilings and massive *stalagmites* growing up to meet them, not to mention an array of bizarre creatures.

These early humans didn't have much time to think about how the icicle-like structures might have formed or why the ghostly pale animals they encountered had no eyes. These people lived hard, usually short, lives. Most of their time was spent looking for food, avoiding predators, and raising children.

They had no written language, but they probably enjoyed telling stories. As you know, when a story is told and retold by many different people, the details of the story can change. Over thousands of years, stories about cave creatures were blown way out of proportion. As a result, people living 600 or 700 years ago thought of caves as dark, scary places. Caves in many parts of the world had become the subject of myths and legends.

In Europe, brave knights and princes were sent to kill the ferocious fire-breathing dragons that lived in caves. If anyone doubted the existence of these terrible beasts, all they had to do was listen for a dragon's mighty roar (the sound of a cave stream flowing after a winter thaw) or be on the look out for its

This cave has huge stalactites hanging down from the ceiling as well as impressive stalagmites growing up to meet them. Both features are made of limestone.

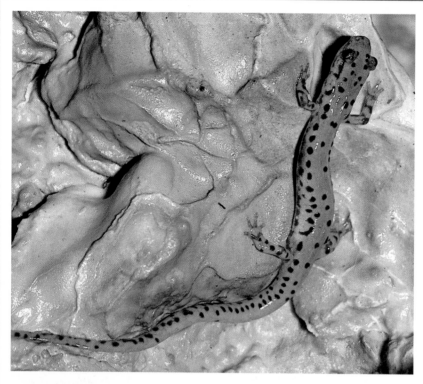

Cave salamanders like this one are found near a cave's entrance zone.

These cave crickets were photographed at a cave in New Jersey.

Cave salamanders like this one are found in a cave's dark zone.

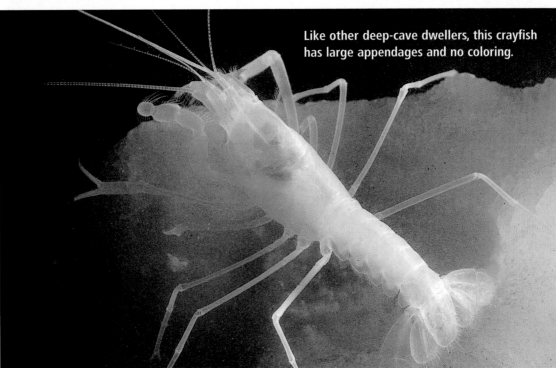

Like other deep-cave dwellers, this crayfish has large appendages and no coloring.

A scientist crawls
through a passage
in Movile Cave.

This earthworm-eating leech is a resident of Movile Cave.

This species of pillbug is found only in Movile Cave.

This pale-colored scorpion is hunting for food in Movile Cave.

A Movile Cave centipede scurries across a rock.

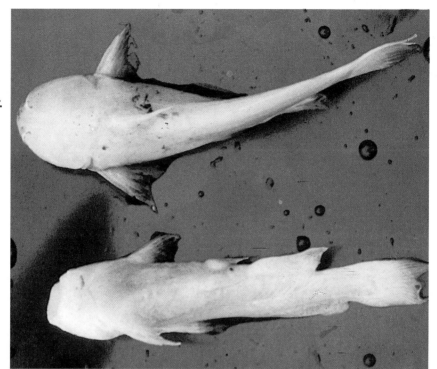

The widemouth blind-cat (above) and the toothless blindcat (below) can be found only in Edward's Aquifer.

This Texas blind salamander is also a resident of Edward's Aquifer.

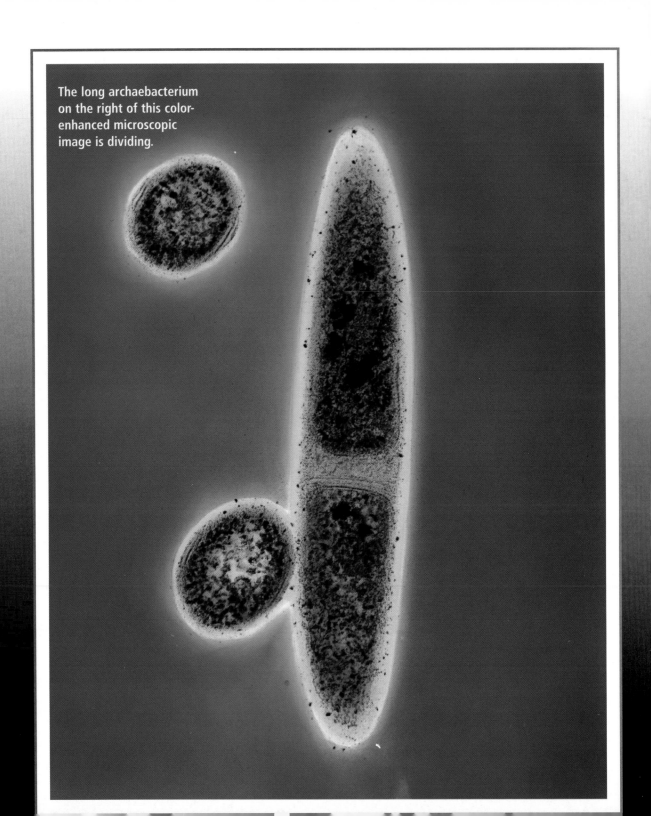

The long archaebacterium on the right of this color-enhanced microscopic image is dividing.

steamy breath (gases rising from an opening between rocks).

The Cave of Cruachan in Ireland was sometimes called the "hell gate of Ireland." According to an Irish tale, every Halloween, fiends and goblins who normally lived underground came out of the cave to kill animals and destroy crops.

In Scandinavian countries, people thought that trolls lived in caves. These gnarled creatures mined precious gems and occasionally kidnapped unsuspecting maidens who wandered too close to a cave. According to these stories, if a troll came into contact with sunlight, it either exploded or turned to stone. That's why people never saw them.

In Medieval mythology, knights battled fierce, fire-breathing, cave-dwelling dragons.

The Wonder of Caves

Eventually, people started exploring caves. They didn't stumble across trolls, goblins, or dragons, but they did find all kinds of life. Many familiar animals can be found close to the entrance of a cave. This part of the cave receives some light, and the conditions are similar to those outside—except that the temperature and humidity vary less. That's why a cave seems cool in the summer and warm in the winter.

The animals that can be found in a cave's entrance zone depend on the cave for protection, either from predators or from the harsher environmental conditions outside. Yet each of these creatures also relies on the world outside the cave for food.

The entrance zone is where bears spend the winter; birds such as swallows, swifts, and phoebes build nests; and leopards and hyenas sleep. Brightly colored salamanders hide in crevices in the walls, and rats stockpile seeds and nuts. A careful observer may spy daddy longlegs scurrying across the floor or brown and yellow cave crickets perching on the walls.

Deeper in the cave are animals that thrive in the dark. Colonies of bats spend the day hanging upside down. At night, they go out in search of prey. Crawling animals such as cockroaches, beetles, amphipods, flatworms, millipedes, and snails also live in this region of the cave, which scientists call the twilight zone.

Except for bats, the creatures found here rarely leave the cave. Yet, it is impossible to overlook the importance of the one animal that awakens each evening, carefully grooms itself, and then flies into the darkness in search of insects, fruit, frogs, small mammals, or even blood. Without bats, the twilight zone ecosystem could not survive.

The smallest creatures—millipedes, beetles, cockroaches, amphipods, and flatworms—feed on bat guano, or drop-

pings. Because no plants can survive in this poorly lit environment, the rich supply of nutrients in the bat dung forms the base of the food chain. The spiders that live in this part of the cave eat smaller insects, while salamanders dine on amphipods and flatworms. When all these animals die, their remains are broken down by decomposers such as cave fungus. In turn, the fungus is a source of food for fungus gnats, which secrete gray spiderlike threads that allow them to scale cave walls in search of food.

At sunset, these round leaf horseshoe bats will leave their cave and search for food all night long.

The Wonder of Caves

Beyond the cave's twilight zone is complete darkness. The creatures that inhabit this dark zone, the *troglobites,* never venture into the light of day. That's why they seem so strange. Most of the animals we are familiar with have eyes so they can see, thick skins so their bodily fluids won't evaporate, colorful feathers or scales so they can blend in with their environment, or thick fur to keep them warm.

Troglobites look very different from animals that live aboveground because they live in a different place and have a different lifestyle. Their world is dark, wet, and warm. They have small, nonfunctional eyes or no eyes at all. Most have larger appendages and antennae than their relatives aboveground so they can feel their way around in the dark.

Because the Sun's burning rays are absent and their predators are blind, the skins of deep cave dwellers have no colorful pigments. As a result, the animals look ghostly white or completely transparent. In some cases, the blood racing through their vessels makes them look slightly pinkish. The cave air is always moist, so they do not need thick skins. And since many troglobites can absorb all the oxygen they need through their thin skins, they have no lungs or gills.

The largest troglobite is the proteus, or blind cave newt. This 12-inch (30-cm)-long creature lives in the caves of eastern Europe. In the Middle Ages, proteus were often killed by adventurous noblemen who believed they were baby dragons.

The proteus has an eel-like body, a triangular head, and a tail that resembles a ship's rudder. These unusual creatures can shrink and expand in response to the availability of food. If food is scarce, this newt may live for up to 3 years without eating.

Like most troglobites, the blind cave newt is pale and has thin skin. Just under its skin are powerful nerve endings that help it navigate, locate prey, and sense the presence of predators. Because these blind creatures are so aware of their surroundings, they scurry to nearby hiding places whenever humans come near. This makes them difficult to observe, and even harder to catch.

Other deep cave dwellers are even more elusive than proteus. That's because they are quite small and can sense danger long before we are able to spot them. Troglobites are small for two reasons. First, they must be able to fit through the cave's low, twisting passages. Such cramped quarters are another reason scientists have trouble studying the darkest regions of many caves. As a result, we know far less about troglobites than the creatures that live closer to cave entrances.

Troglobites are also small because the food supply in a cave's dark zone is limited. There is no sunlight, so no plants grow there. Bats do not roost so far from the cave's entrance, so guano is not readily available.

What do the creatures eat? Maybe you think the answer has something to do with chemoautotrophs, but it doesn't. Actually, the ultimate source of food in a cave's dark zone has more in common with the marine snow that feeds the inhabitants of the deep ocean.

In the deep sea, debris floats down from above. In a cave's dark zone, waste material is swept along by underground streams and deposited in quiet pools. These streams bring plant debris from the world outside. In some cases, they also deliver small quantities of bat guano from the cave's twilight zone. Without the food supplied by the part of the world where photosynthesis occurs, deep cave dwellers would starve. Thus, they too are dependent on the Sun. Troglobites are also dependent on flowing water. While the outer regions of caves are usually dry, the dark zone must still be "active"— have running water—for life to exist there.

In the dark zone, guano and plant debris are a source of food for a variety of bacteria, *protoctists,* and animals—

wingless beetles, microscopic waterfleas, and nimble springtails. These creatures, in turn, are eaten by amphipods, copepods, planarians, isopods, and cave crayfish. At the top of the food chain are salamanders with their eyelids fused shut and blind cavefish that sense their environment through nerve endings located in their lips and along the sides and tops of their heads. When cave animals die, bacteria and other decomposers derive nutrients from their bodies, and in turn, become a source of food for animals close to the bottom of the food chain.

Despite the challenges of studying troglobites, patient cave scientists—called *speleologists*—have been able to work

Speleologists often use elaborate equipment to study the deep recesses of caves.

out the intricacies of deep cave food chains. But speleologists are interested in more than just that. They are also working to understand the steps in another complicated process—cave formation.

THE BEGINNING OF A CAVE

A cave is any air-filled underground cavity that has an opening to the surface and is large enough to be examined in some way by humans. There are several types of caves—lava caves, ice caves, wind caves, and *solution caves.* Each type of cave is formed in a different way. The most common type of cave—the type you are probably picturing in your mind right now—is the solution cave.

A solution cave forms when soluble bedrock such as limestone is dissolved by water. It is not actually the water that does the dissolving, however; it is chemicals in the water. In most cases, carbon dioxide, CO_2, is the culprit. Rain absorbs some of this carbon dioxide as it falls through the atmosphere. Rainwater picks up additional carbon dioxide as it seeps through soil and decaying matter. The result is a weak carbonic acid. Soda pop is one example of a carbonic acid. If you drop a piece of limestone into a glass of Coca-Cola®, the limestone will slowly disintegrate and dissolve. Once in a while, a solution cave is formed by water containing sulfuric acid. This water wells up from below to erode the bedrock.

In either case, there must be a way for the water to enter the soluble bedrock layer. Geologists know that most of Earth's underground limestone layers were once ocean floor. Most limestone, a type of *sedimentary rock,* is actually the compressed remains of countless seashells. These shells

A solution cave forms very gradually as underground water dissolves layers of sedimentary rock.

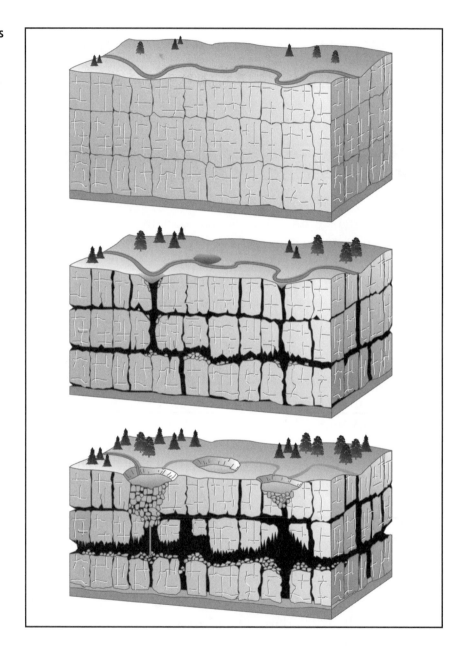

were made of *calcium carbonate,* which was secreted by the sea creatures that once lived inside the shells.

When the shellfish died, the animals decayed, but their protective homes did not. Instead, the empty shells fell to the ocean floor. Over time, layer upon layer of calcium carbonate shells piled up. As the weight of the uppermost shells and other sediments exerted pressure on the shells below, solid limestone formed.

Eventually the ocean dried up, but the layers of limestone were left behind. Other materials were deposited on top of the limestone, and soon the limestone layer was buried deep below the surface. At some point, geologic activity in the region lifted and tilted some of the limestone layers. Because the material at the edges of the sedimentary layers is not tightly packed, water trickling down toward the *water table* moves into the rock and begins to dissolve it. In many cases, volcanic activity and earthquakes create faults and cracks in the limestone. Additional water can enter the sedimentary rock through these fractures.

Over thousands of years, the carbonic acid solution slowly eats away at the limestone. The cracks and faults become wider, allowing water to flow through more quickly. The limestone that comes into contact with the underground stream breaks down more rapidly. As time passes, rock that was once fractured is completely dissolved and replaced by a large water-filled cavern.

At some point after a cave begins to form, climate changes on the surface cause the water table to drop below the level of the cave or geological shifting raises the cave above the water table. As a result, part of the underground cavern is filled with air.

Eventually, the water may cut an entrance. The cave may also open to the surface when part of the cave collapses, forming a vertical entrance. Sometimes a cave is first exposed to the outside world by humans—workers drilling a well or digging the foundation of a new building.

The Wonder of Caves

In 1986, Romanian construction workers discovered an underground cave that had been sealed off from the rest of the world for more than 5.5 million years. The uppermost regions of the cave are about 60 feet (18 m) below a cornfield. The site is near the city of Mangalia, 10 miles (16 km) from the Bulgarian border.

When scientists began to study Movile Cave in 1989, they found walls covered with grayish white mats of fungi that look like waterlogged toilet paper, leeches that slurp down worms whole, and long-legged spiders that have no use for webs. These astounding spiders rely on their keen hearing and sense of smell to chase down small prey.

In all, scientists identified 33 unique species of small animals in the cave, which measures 800 feet (240 m) by 160 feet (50 m). Among these bizarre cave creatures are four types of pill bugs, six species of springtails, four kinds of spiders, two types of pseudoscorpions and one water scorpion, a bristletail worm, and a millipede. The largest cave inhabitant is a 2-inch (5-cm)-long centipede.

The creatures that call Movile Cave home have a lot in common with the organisms found in caves all over the world. They are pale or transparent, blind or eyeless, and have thin skins. Yet despite their external similarity to other troglobites, the animals in Movile Cave also have something in common with the organisms living in a very different environment—the hydrothermal vents scattered along the world's midocean ridges. While the inhabitants of most caves feed on bat guano and decayed plants swept down from the surface, the animals in Movile Cave have a diet similar to the creatures found in vent communities on the ocean floor.

Microorganisms living on the walls and floating on the water that partially fills the cave are at the base of the Movile Cave food chain. Like vent microorganisms, these tiny cave creatures get the energy they need to grow and develop from a chemical source.

No one knows exactly where the chemicals—sulfides, methane, and ammonium ions—come from. Because the water in the cave is relatively warm, scientists believe that it may be circulating to the crust's deepest regions. During this long journey through many types of rock, the water may absorb the chemicals that fuel chemosynthesis. The carbon compounds produced during this process are the nutritional source for the entire ecosystem.

Movile Cave is the first known terrestrial ecosystem in which no animals eat photosynthetic organisms. Like vent bacteria, the bacteria in Movile Cave are not completely inde-

This spider was discovered in Movile Cave.

The Wonder of Caves

pendent of the Sun's rays. They do need a tiny amount of oxygen. This oxygen, which leaks from Earth's surface through microscopic cracks in the cave's limestone walls, is ultimately a byproduct of photosynthesis.

HOW MOVILE CAVE FORMED

Scientists believe that the cave dwellers' ancestors lived at a time when the climate of Europe was similar to that of a tropical rain forest today. When some unknown event suddenly caused the environment to become much colder and drier, the organisms took refuge in the cave, which was kept warm by water bubbling up from deep cracks in Earth's crust. At that time, the cave's entrance was at sea level, so creatures that could adapt to their new dark habitat survived and reproduced.

Eventually, geological shifting in the area sealed the cave off from the surface. Now the organisms had another environmental change to face—an almost complete lack of oxygen. As time passed, concentrations of gases toxic to most terrestrial animals increased. Today, there is ten times more carbon dioxide in the cave than on Earth's surface. The air is also full of sulfide compounds and methane. Many creatures rose to the environmental challenge by evolving biological mechanisms that allowed them to thrive in these harsh conditions. The descendants of these organisms lived undisturbed for millions of years, until 1986 when humans stumbled across the site.

As the cave's microorganisms carried out chemosynthesis, they may have done more than just provide their fellow cave creatures with energy. As you learned in Chapter 4, one of the products of the reaction that precedes chemosynthesis is a sulfate ion, SO_4^{-2}. When this ion combines with two hydrogen ions, H^+, the result is sulfuric acid, H_2SO_4.

$$SO_4^{-2} + 2\ H^+ \rightarrow H_2SO_4$$

Sulfuric acid is a powerful chemical that eats away at the cave's walls, which are made of limestone or calcium carbonate, $CaCO_3$.

Over the centuries, this chemical reaction has hollowed out the great underground chamber that is now called Movile Cave. Scientists know that this reaction is occurring because the walls of the cave are lined with gypsum. The chemical name for gypsum is calcium sulfate, $CaSO_4 \cdot 2\ H_2O$. Calcium sulfate is one of the products of the reaction between calcium carbonate and sulfuric acid.

$$H_2SO_4 + CaCO_3 + 2\ H^+ \rightarrow CaSO_4 \cdot 2\ H_2O + CO_2$$

BEYOND THE CAVE

Movile Cave may be a small part of an *aquifer,* an underground layer of rock that contains water. One goal of early research conducted at the cave was to prove that the underground springs that spill into Movile Cave are truly isolated from water at the surface. By measuring concentrations of various chemicals in water collected from the deep springs that supply water to the cave and water collected close to the surface, it was possible to show that the water comes from different sources.

This finding comes as no big surprise to Thomas Kane, a professor of biology at the University of Cincinnati in Ohio. "People have known since the days of the Greeks and Romans that the spring water here was unusual," he said.[1] This water, which has very high levels of sulfur, has been in demand at health spas around the world for centuries.

CHAPTER SIX

A Look Below the Surface

There is not so much Life as talk of Life,
as a general thing. Had we the first
intimation of the Definition of Life, the
calmest of us would be Lunatics!

Emily Dickinson, letter to Mrs. Holland, c. 1881

Another aquifer—located about 8,500 miles (13,700 km) from Movile Cave—appears to be the home of a completely different, but equally bizarre, group of organisms. Below the soil of south-central Texas, water meanders through a series of limestone caverns and channels known as Edward's Aquifer. Some regions of the limestone aquifer are more than 2,000 feet (610 m) below ground level.

There are no caves associated with this aquifer. The only openings to the surface are the hundreds of wells that supply more than 1 million people with water. Edward's Aquifer is the only source of water for San Antonio, the ninth-largest city in the United States.

Local lore is full of tall tales of the aquifer's curious creatures. The first documented sighting of extraordinary animals is from 1895. The U.S. Fish Commission drilled a deep hole to get water for a new fish hatchery, and workers were startled when several pale invertebrates and a blind salamander that looked like a long-legged tadpole with gills surfaced.

A few years later, a strange fish popped out of a 1,010-foot (308-m)-deep well in San Antonio. The ghostly pale fish had red lips; razor-sharp, paper-thin jaws on the underside of its head; and no eyes at all. It was a toothless, blind catfish, or blindcat.

Scientists now know that this fish's unusual jaws are used to scrape microbial or fungal mats off the ledges and floors along the 152-mile (242-km)-long expanse of twisting tunnels and caverns within Edward's Aquifer.

All blindcats have an adaptation similar to one that evolved in deep-sea animals—fatty sacs that help them regulate their body pressure and remain buoyant. This is not surprising since the creatures living in both environments must be able to deal with tremendous pressure.

During the early to mid-1900s, there were isolated reports of tiny snails and assorted crustaceans in local wells and a blindcat in a roadside ditch. Many other specimens went unreported. That's not too remarkable. After all, they were unwelcome visitors, intruders in a supposedly pure water supply. A number of people recall that when the water tower at a food processing plant in San Antonio was drained in 1964, fifty blindcats were discovered. The water in the tower had come from a 1,410-foot (430-m)-deep well.

In 1976, Glenn Longley noticed a few white invertebrates wiggling in spillways from the well on the campus of Southwest Texas State University, in San Marcos. He was intrigued by these tiny creatures. That night he made a trap with a coat hanger and a pair of his wife's pantyhose. The next day he placed his simple apparatus over the well's outflow pipe.

Longley was amazed by the number and variety of small creatures he captured. "I didn't have any idea that such an extensive community could exist so deep underground," says Longley. "It's possibly the world's most unique groundwater ecosystem."[1]

Between 1976 and 1981, Longley trapped organisms from twenty-two local wells and several nearby springs. He identified at least forty new species of small animals—several snails, two one-eyed copepods, an ostracod, a beetle, a number of amphipods, and a planarian. Like the creatures found deep within caves, these organisms had no pigmentation and lacked functioning eyes.

Samples from Edward's Aquifer are collected from wells.

HOW EDWARD'S AQUIFER FORMED

The aquifer's history goes back hundreds of millions of years. The limestone layers that house the aquifer were slowly deposited as ancient seas dried up and refilled. When fresh-water crept between and into the layers of sedimentary rock, it formed a series of irregularly shaped underground caverns.

About 10 million years ago, geologic activity created a fault zone. In the process, some of the limestone layers were lifted above the sea that covered the area and formed a plateau to the north and west of the fault. The limestone layers to the southeast of the fault remained underwater, and over thousands of years, marine sediment buried them. Today, part of the aquifer is below the limestone plateau and part is below a coastal plain that formed when the sea finally receded.

Near the fault, the aquifer is close to the surface of the ground. Runoff from rainstorms seeps downward, carrying organic material such as leaves and small twigs into some regions of the aquifer. But the portion of the aquifer that is home to the creatures that Longley studies is much farther below the surface. Although water does eventually reach these depths, decaying plant material does not.

THOUGHTS ABOUT FOOD

So if plants do not provide this ecosystem with fuel, what does? The truth is, no one can answer this question. Scientists know less about these creatures and their food chain than about vent organisms or the inhabitants of Movile Cave because they cannot explore the world firsthand. Such an investigation would threaten the water's purity and might make it undrinkable. This would be disastrous for San

Antonio, San Marcos, and more than a dozen smaller communities in south-central Texas. Despite these limitations, scientists have been able to piece together some information about the creatures living in the aquifer.

The Amphipods' Story

Scientists were surprised to discover that twelve separate species of amphipods live in Edward's Aquifer. According to John R. Holsinger, a biologist at Old Dominion University in Norfolk, Virginia, it is unusual for so many different species of amphipods to live in a single ecosystem. It is especially startling that such diversity exists in the aquifer because the variety and quantity of food is limited.[2]

By studying each species closely, scientists have discovered why there are so many different types of amphipods in Edward's Aquifer. Each species has a different type of mouth and its own food sources. Each species also acts and moves differently. Some walk along the cavern floor in search of food. Others swim or float in the water and filter feed. Still others cling to the cavern walls. As a result, the amphipods do not compete for available food.

The amphipods may have evolved separately during eras when geological activity isolated small groups of amphipods, so that each group developed differently. Later, additional geologic activity may have created new channels and brought several different groups of amphipods back together.

Close study of the amphipods has led scientists to believe that different species have very different origins and probably moved into the aquifer at different times. About 80 percent of the amphipods seem to have saltwater origins. Their ancestors lived in shallow marine and brackish waters. Others seem most closely related to fossils of animals that lived in an ancient body of saltwater called the Sea of Tethys. Millions of years ago,

When new wells are dug, a slimy discharge filled with a variety of microorganisms sometimes gushes out along with the water. These tiny creatures are probably at the base of the ecosystem's food chain, but it isn't clear how *they* obtain nutri-

this sea covered what are now the Caribbean and Mediterranean regions of the world. Still others seem to have had ancestors that lived in deep water. Their closest living relatives inhabit the Indo-West Pacific. The remaining 20 percent of amphipods in Edward's Aquifer descended from an ancestor that lived in a freshwater ecosystem with a climate like that of the United States today.

Like the inhabitants of Movile Cave, the amphipods probably retreated into the aquifer in an effort to survive during a time when their environment was going through changes. Perhaps the climate was warming up or cooling down, or perhaps the salinity of the water they lived in was changing. By adapting to the aquifer environment, they were able to avoid extinction.

Amphipods are not the only aquifer inhabitants to have ancestors that lived in other parts of the world. The water beetle species found there has Eurasian origins. It has little in common with American species of beetles. One of the isopods appears to come from what is now Mexico. Other organisms have close relatives living in the West Indies or the Mediterranean region.

How is it possible that the organisms now living below Texas have origins in half a dozen different places? The most likely explanation is that, over thousands or even millions of years, plate tectonics carried Texas to different regions of the globe and brought it in contact with a variety of different seas and land masses. At each encounter, the aquifer gained a couple of new inhabitants.

ents. They may be able to manufacture the materials they need to survive from the carbon that makes up old *organic matter*, including oil. During periods of drought, some wells ooze oil. It is also possible that the deepest regions of the aquifer may contain enough ancient carbon to feed the creatures at the base of the community's food chain. Scientists envision limestone walls covered with a variety of microbes feasting on fossilized organic matter within the layers of marine sediment.

The microorganisms are a source of food for a variety of aquifer organisms, including amphipods, copepods, snails, shrimp, and blindcats. Many of these creatures are found throughout the aquifer. Blind shrimp are almost everywhere. Scientists believe that they may expand their range during eras when high water or geologic shifts make migration possible. Amphipods are also scattered throughout most of the aquifer's deep regions. Different species of amphipods have different eating habits, patterns of movement, and behaviors, so they do not compete with each other.

An amphipod from Edward's Aquifer

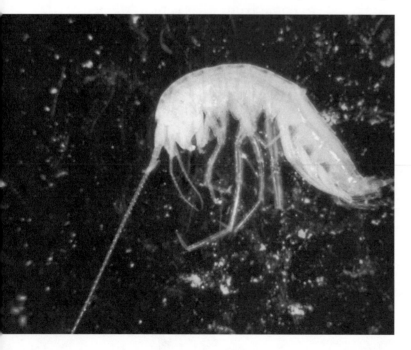

A second species of blindcat, the widemouth blindcat, has a more varied diet. It eats many kinds of organisms, including smaller toothless blindcats. Widemouth blindcats are at the top of the aquifer ecosystem in the San Antonio area. Because no ecosystem can support too many predators, other carnivores live in other regions of the aquifer. Salamanders, for example, dominate the portion of the aquifer near San Marcos.

The salamanders living in Edward's Aquifer look very different from the salamanders found hiding under rotten logs or crawling through the leaf litter that carpets the forest floor. They have undergone incredible evolutionary changes to adapt to their underground habitat. They are blind, pale, and breathe through gills all their lives. They are also part of a very unconventional food chain.

These salamanders, and all their aquifer neighbors, live in an unusual, and possibly unique, ecosystem. Like the creatures that live in caves and the deep sea, they never see the light of day. In fact, direct exposure to the Sun's ultraviolet rays would kill them. Yet as far removed as these organisms are from sunlight, they could not survive without solar energy. The creatures in Edward's Aquifer need oxygen to maintain their bodies, and oxygen is a byproduct of photosynthesis.

By now, you're probably beginning to think that every organism on Earth somehow relies on the burning star at the center of our solar system. After all, every creature mentioned so far depends on the Sun. You have considered organisms living in forests and wetlands, coral reefs and the deep sea, caves and limestone aquifers. Is there any other place to look? As it turns out, there is—inside rocks.

In the late 1980s, a group of researchers in South Carolina discovered a community of microbes living in hot sedimentary rock 1,640 feet (500 m) below the surface. In 1993, another group of scientists working in eastern Virginia found yet another species of bacteria 8,800 feet (2,700 m) underground. Although these microorganisms live in darkness, they too need the Sun. They dine on organic compounds—oil and fossilized materials, just like the smallest members of the Edward's Aquifer ecosystem.

In 1995, Todd O. Stevens and James P. McKinley, geochemists at Pacific West Laboratory in Richland, Washington, found signs of microscopic life in basalt rock more than 3,200 feet (1,000 m) underground. By this time, identifying microbes in rock was no big deal. But the tiny creatures in the Washington rock were very different from the ones found in South Carolina and Virginia. Rather than living in sedimentary rock, they lived in basalt—a type of volcanic *igneous rock*. Volcanic rock is made of solidified lava. It is extremely hard and contains no organic material. Scientists began asking a very important question: What were these microbes eating?

The answer startled scientists around the world. Like the chemoautotrophs that live around deep-sea vents and in Movile Cave, these microorganisms do not depend on the Sun for energy. Using only water and rock, these amazing organisms produce all the materials they need to grow and reproduce. The process requires no oxygen. These creatures seem to require absolutely nothing from the Sun. Here, at last, is strong evidence that an ecosystem can, in fact, exist without the Sun.

ENERGY FROM ROCK

The rock that these amazing subterranean creatures call home is located far below a portion of the Columbia River basin in Washington. More than 7 million years ago, geologic activity in the area tore open a section of crust, and tons of sizzling lava poured out. As time passed, the lava hardened, forming basalt. Sedimentary rock was deposited on top of the basalt, and pressure within the crust forced the basalt to fold over and break up.

Today, rainwater that has picked up carbon dioxide as it falls through the atmosphere mixes with the basalt deep within Earth's crust. In a process that scientists do not fully understand, the mixture of water and crushed basalt releases hydrogen.

Subterranean archaebacteria called *methanogens* obtain the energy they need to grow and reproduce by combining the hydrogen, H_2, from basalt with the carbon dioxide, CO_2, from rainwater that has trickled down from the surface. The products of this reaction are methane, CH_4, and water, H_2O.

$$CO_2 + 4 H_2 \rightarrow CH_4 + 2 H_2O$$

Methanogens are also found in a variety of other oxygen-poor environments, including marshes and swamps, sewage, and the digestive tracts of cud-chewing animals—cows, sheep, and goats. Unlike their subterranean cousins, these methanogens get hydrogen and carbon dioxide from the bacterial decomposers that break down organic matter. Methanogenic archaebacteria are not the only creatures living deep underground. They are a source of food for other microorganisms. As anaerobic bacteria, they don't need oxygen either.

ONE THING LEADS TO ANOTHER

More recently, a group of Swedish researchers have found a similar subterranean community of archaebacteria and other types of bacteria living in granite 1,300 feet (400 m) below the surface. Because granite is one of the most common rocks in Earth's crust, some scientists think there could be as much life

A Look Below the Surface

hidden belowground as there is on the surface. In fact, Thomas Gold, a researcher at Cornell University in Ithaca, New York, believes that the weight of all subterranean microbes could equal that of all organisms living on the surface.[3]

The discovery of subterranean life has captured the interest and imagination of scientists all over the world. It has also led them to ask a host of new questions: How common are subterranean communities? How long have these ecosystems existed? If microbes can survive deep below Earth's surface, could they live under the surface of other planets? The answers to these questions are years, perhaps even decades, away. But scientists know where to start looking for solutions—archaebacteria.

CHAPTER SEVEN

Archaebacteria: A Closer Look

Here, Gentlemen, you have the notes
that I have kept about my observations:
in making which I said to myself, how many
creatures are still unbeknown to us,
and how little do we yet understand!

Antonie van Leeuwenhoek

No one was more excited about the discovery of archaebacteria in basalt rock more than 3,200 feet (1,000 m) underground than Carl Woese, an evolutionist at the University of Illinois in Urbana. It made him think back to the day in 1977 when he made a startling discovery of his own. Before it is possible to appreciate the significance of what Woese found, you need to know something about *taxonomy*—the identification, naming, and classification of living things into groups. One of the largest schemes for classifying living things was developed by a Swedish botanist named Carolus Linnaeus in the 1700s.

---

89   **Archaebacteria: A Closer Look**

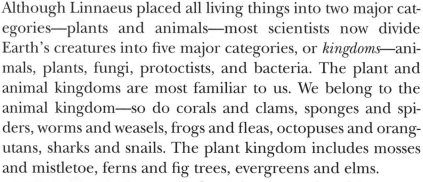

Although Linnaeus placed all living things into two major categories—plants and animals—most scientists now divide Earth's creatures into five major categories, or *kingdoms*—animals, plants, fungi, protoctists, and bacteria. The plant and animal kingdoms are most familiar to us. We belong to the animal kingdom—so do corals and clams, sponges and spiders, worms and weasels, frogs and fleas, octopuses and orangutans, sharks and snails. The plant kingdom includes mosses and mistletoe, ferns and fig trees, evergreens and elms.

Swedish scientist Carolus Linnaeus developed the system modern scientists use to name, identify, and classify all living things.

Organisms are placed in a particular group because their physical traits, behavioral patterns, and chemical processes are more similar to those of the other members of that group than they are to the organisms in other groups. Here's an example: An ant is more similar to an aardvark than it is to an apple tree, so the ant and the aardvark have been placed in the same kingdom. The common ancestor of the ant and the aardvark lived more recently than the common ancestor of the ant and the apple tree.

Of course, an ant is not all that similar to an aardvark. An ant has much more in common with a grasshopper that it does with an aardvark. That's why within each kingdom, there are additional subgroups of organisms. An ant and an aardvark both belong to the same kingdom, but they belong to different *phyla*. Because an aardvark has an internal skeleton and a backbone, it belongs to the chordate phylum. An ant belongs to the arthropod phylum, which includes all insects, spiders, and crustaceans (lobsters, crabs, shrimp, and more). An aardvark and an ant can be further classified as belonging to other, even more specific, subgroups—*class, order, family, genus,* and species.

A somewhat similar system is used to group soldiers in the U.S. Army. A corps, the highest level of organization, is composed of several divisions. The 10,000 to 20,000 soldiers in each division perform a particular type of work (airborne, armored, infantry, etc.). The next subcategory, the brigade, usually has 3,000 to 5,000 soldiers who can be subdivided into a number of battalions. Each battalion has 500 to 1,000 members. A company, which has about 150 soldiers, is made of three or four platoons of about 40 soldiers each. The smallest subgroup, a squad, has about 10 members.

An army squad can be compared to a taxonomic species. Of course the major difference between the classification systems used by scientists and the army is that living things are grouped according to biological and chemical similarities, soldiers are not.

An aardvark belongs to the mammal class. Because humans are also mammals, an aardvark is more closely related to you than it is to an ant. Humans belong to the primate order, the Hominidae family, the *Homo* genus, and the sapiens species. An organism's scientific name, which is always written in italics, is a combination of its genus name and its species name. Our scientific name is *Homo sapiens.*

All plants and animals can be grouped according to this system—so can fungi, protoctists, and bacteria. The fungus kingdom includes molds, mushrooms and toadstools, and

Many protoctists, including this diatom, are a single cell.

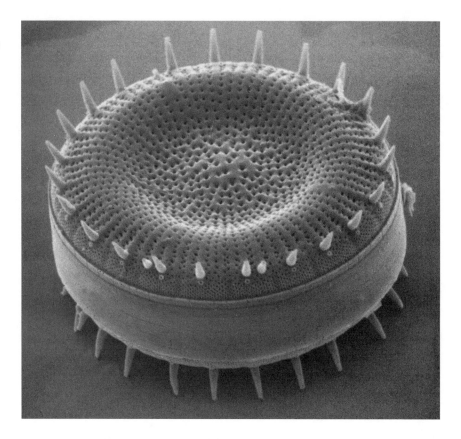

yeasts. The protoctist kingdom includes a wide variety of organisms. Some—the *protists*—consist of one cell or just a few cells. This group includes most amebas, diatoms, and ciliates. Giant seaweeds, such a kelp, slime molds that sometimes creep over entire trees, and fuzzy water molds on the surfaces of decaying seeds are protoctists, too. Bacteria are even smaller and simpler than protoctists.

Many years ago, scientists realized that bacteria are different from all other life forms. When they looked at bacterial cells under the microscope, they noticed that they do not have nuclei. A cell's nucleus is a subcompartment surrounded by a membrane. Inside is the cell's DNA. In bacteria, DNA floats around the cell. To emphasize the importance of this difference, scientists divided all living things into two super-104kingdoms—the prokarya, which includes only bacteria, and eukarya, which includes everything else.

BIZARRE BACTERIA

Scientists know a great deal about the eukarya, especially plants and animals. Humans have been studying these creatures since ancient times. We know far less about the prokarya. It was not until the late 1600s that the microscope was invented and scientists like Antonie van Leeuwenhoek and Robert Hooke first peeked into the microworld.

Over the years, microscope technology has come a long way. Today, there are electron microscopes that can magnify specimens 100,000 to 150,000 times. The microscope has allowed us to appreciate the diversity and importance of microorganisms. Some break down organic matter. Others provide more complex organisms with food to eat and oxygen to breathe. A few cause fatal diseases.

By the 1970s, scientists knew enough about microorganisms to recognize a complete oddball. Scattered here and there among the scientific literature were a few reports of baffling bacteria that seemed to be the exception to every biological rule. These strange creatures somehow managed to eke out a meager existence in some of the world's most extreme environments—places that were too hot, too acidic, under too much pressure, or had too little oxygen for most organisms.

Because they seem to prefer some of the most hostile environments on Earth—places that were once thought unable to support life—scientists originally believed that they must be rare. They were considered strange exceptions to the rules of nature. As a result, they were never studied as a group. Whenever someone discovered one of these curious creatures, they named it and then forgot about it. Most scientists just ignored them altogether.

Carl Woese was not like most scientists. He was intrigued by these mysterious microbes. After comparing the creatures to each other and to other organisms, he realized that these were no ordinary bacteria. In fact, in 1977, he announced that this unusual group of creatures, which he called archaea or archaebacteria, has as much in common with eukarya—protoctists, plants, fungi, and animals—as it does with other types of bacteria. To emphasize the importance of his finding, Woese divided the bacterial world into two groups: the archaebacteria and the *eubacteria*. Like other bacteria, archaebacteria lack nuclei. However, the ribosomes and many of the genes of archaebacteria are more like those of eukarya.

Other scientists were hesitant to accept Woese's work. Were these mysterious microbes bacteria or not? Microscopes could not provide the answer. They could only provide scientists with information about the microbes' relative sizes and shapes. This was not enough to assign these small creatures to taxonomic groups. According to Roger Stainer of the University of California, Berkeley, "It was as if you went to a zoo and had no way of telling the lions from the elephants from the orangutans—or any of these from the trees."[1] What scientists needed was information about the microbes' chemical makeup and genetics. The tools for obtaining this information did not become available until the 1990s.

In 1996, a group of scientists led by Carol J. Bult of the Institute for Genomic Research in Rockville, Maryland, announced that her team had sequenced the entire *genome* of *Methanococcus jannaschii*, an archaebacterium recovered from a hydrothermal chimney on the floor of the Pacific Ocean.

Methanococcus jannaschii was the fifth organism—and the second bacterium—to be entirely sequenced. Scientists decided to study it because it is so unusual. "It's like something out of science fiction," said J. Craig Venter, genome scientist and president of the Institute for Genomic Research. "Not so long ago, no one would have believed you if you'd told them such organisms existed on Earth."[2] After all, how many creatures could live in a 201°F (94°C) bath?

The researchers found that some of the genes that make up the DNA of *Methanococcus jannaschii* are similar to those of eubacteria. Others, however, are more like the genes of eukarya. Some even resembled those of yeasts and humans. Based on these results, many researchers thought that archaebacteria should be classified as neither prokarya nor eukaya. Perhaps, they suggested, these microbes should be considered a completely separate branch on the tree of life. This idea was—and still is—very controversial.

By the summer of 1998, more than a dozen microbes had been sequenced. As scientists studied and compared these genomes, they found some big surprises. Some microorganisms that are classified as eubacteria based on their physical characteristics contained genes that code for proteins more closely related to those of archaebacteria. In other cases, bacteria genes appeared to be more similar to those of plants and animals than to those of other bacteria. This finding confirmed the idea that it is not uncommon for microbes to steal genes from other creatures. Genes can come from foods the bacteria eat or can be swapped between bacteria. In fact, many bacteria trade genetic material as casually as 10-year-olds trade baseball cards.

Scientists who study plants and animals know that if two organisms have very similar DNA, they are closely related. That is why we believe, for example, that humans are closely related to chimpanzees and gorillas. Scientists who study microorganisms know that bacteria accept DNA from their surroundings much more readily than plants or animals. Two bacteria with similar genes may be as closely related as humans and chimps or as distantly related as toads and tulips.

A Look at DNA

DNA is a molecule that carries instructions for building the proteins that allow an organism to grow and function. It is located inside the cells of every living thing. In the 1950s, scientists built the first model of a DNA molecule. This structure looked like a twisting ladder. The legs of the ladder are made of a repeating units of deoxyribose sugar and phosphate. Each rung of the ladder consists of two *nucleotide bases* that are bonded together. There are four kinds of bases—adenine (A), thymine (T), guanine (G), and cytosine (C). Adenine only forms bonds with thymine, and guanine only forms bonds with cytosine.

A gene is a segment of DNA that has all the information needed to build a single protein. It is like an architect's blueprint. Some genes are several hundred nucleotide bases long; others are hundreds of thousands of bases long. A human's DNA has about 3 billion nucleotide bases and about 100,000 genes. Most organisms have much less DNA than humans. *Methanococcus jannaschii,* the archaebacteria collected from a hydrothermal vent on the ocean floor, has only 1,738 genes.

The order, or sequence, of bases in an organism's DNA provides cells with the information they need to make amino acids, which are linked together to form proteins. Cells read DNA's sequence as a series of three-letter words. Each triplet of nucleotide bases "codes" for a specific amino acid. For example, the sequence TATGGTGTTTCC would be read as four triplets: TAT GGT GTT TCC. The triplet TAT is a com-

So far, genome sequencing had provided scientists with a wealth of knowledge about bacteria, but it has failed to answer the questions they have been asking for decades. Are archaebacteria really bacteria? And, if so, how do they fit into the big picture? How are they related to all other living things?

mand to obtain the amino acid tyrosine. GGT codes for glycine; GTT codes for valine; and TCC codes for serine. The resulting protein would include tryrosine, glycine, valine, and serine.

When scientists "sequence" an organism's DNA, they determine the exact order of all its nucleotide bases. Once they know the order of bases, they can figure out what types of proteins the organism uses to carry out cellular functions. They can also compare the organism's genes to those of other creatures.

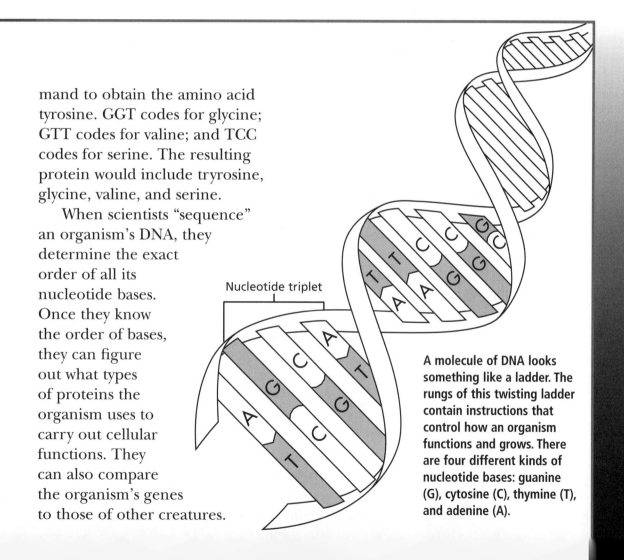

Nucleotide triplet

A molecule of DNA looks something like a ladder. The rungs of this twisting ladder contain instructions that control how an organism functions and grows. There are four different kinds of nucleotide bases: guanine (G), cytosine (C), thymine (T), and adenine (A).

According to an idea recently proposed by Lynn Margulis of the University of Massachusetts, Amherst, and Karlene V. Schwartz of the University of Massachusetts, Boston, the answer can be found by studying the evolution of life on Earth. Their ideas will be discussed in more detail in Chapter 8.

WHY ARCHAEBACTERIA ARE SPECIAL

There are three types of archaebacteria—the methanogens, the thermophiles, and the halophiles. The methanogens, which were mentioned in Chapter 6, live in a variety of habitats inhospitable to us—deep below Earth's surface; in bogs, marshes, swamps, and stagnant ponds; inside the intestines of people, cows, sheep, and goats; on decaying teeth; and in oxygen-depleted sewer water. The thermophiles thrive in hot, sulfur-laden environments such as hot springs and hydrothermal vent communities. They were discussed briefly in Chapter 4. Both methanogens and thermophiles live in oxygen-poor environments. Halophiles are different—they need oxygen to survive. Halophiles live in extremely salty environments and carry out a peculiar form of photosynthesis. These archaebacteria are abundant in seaside salt flats and at commercial salt-making facilities. Some grow in the Dead Sea.

Archaebacteria have special *enzymes* that allow them to flourish in extreme environments. The molecules of most living things would collapse and break down in such hostile habitats. Archaebacteria are biological weirdos for other reasons, too. Some make their own food and generate energy from inorganic chemical ingredients, such as carbon dioxide and hydrogen sulfide. Oxygen, the substance that makes life possible for most organisms, is toxic to two groups of these tiny creatures—it kills them.

In the last few decades, scientists have come to realize that Earth has many extreme environments—the deep sea, hydrothermal vents, hot springs, caves and aquifers cut off from the surface, and subterranean rocks. Archaebacteria, as well as eubacteria, can be found in all these places. The more time researchers spend looking for archaebacteria, the more they find. Recently, many archaebacteria have been found in environments that are far from extreme. "Suddenly [these] organisms that had been relegated to weirdo environments turn out to do fine in normal habitats," says Jed Fuhrman, a microbiologist at the University of Southern California in Los Angeles. "You just have to look for them the right way."[3]

Archaebacteria may actually account for half of all the biomass in the world. Some live in ocean waters off the coast of southern California. One-third of the microbes in surface waters off the coast of Antarctica are archaebacteria. They are the dominant type of microorganism in the deep ocean. And there are nearly forty kinds living in a single hot spring in Yellowstone National Park. Two of these hot spring archaebacteria are among the most primitive organisms on Earth. They are the direct descendants of microbes that lived 3.5 billion years ago.

Archaebacteria live in extreme environments, such as this hot spring in Yellowstone National Park.

Archaebacteria: A Closer Look

The Origin of Life

The truth is out there.

Astronomers believe that our solar system began forming about 5 billion years ago. At first, the Sun was surrounded by a huge, flat, rotating disk made of countless tiny bits of dust. When these dust grains collided, they often stuck together. As more and more particles combined, large masses of rock and ice called *planetesimals* formed. Eventually, these planetesimals developed into planets, comets, and asteroids.

One of these planetesimals became Earth. By 4.5 billion years ago, Earth was revolving around the Sun. During the next 500 million years, the crust cooled enough to solidify. No one knows exactly how life began or developed on our planet.

According to the theory that has traditionally been most popular, a series of random chemical reactions powered by lightning or ultraviolet radiation from the Sun produced stable molecules that could reproduce themselves in a warm ocean. This idea was developed by graduate student Stanley L. Miller and his advisor, Nobel Prize winner Harold C. Urey, at Columbia University in 1953. They based their theory on an experiment they had done in their lab.

They heated an airtight apparatus containing water and gases common in ancient Earth's oceans—hydrogen, ammonia, and methane. Miller zapped the mixture with electrical sparks meant to simulate lightning. A week later, the gases had formed a dark, slimy substance that contained amino acids and other important organic compounds. More recently, other scientists have shown that adenine, one of the four nucleotide bases in DNA, can form spontaneously when ammonia combines with methane.

Stanley L. Miller, shown here, and Harold C. Urey developed an influential theory to explain how life on Earth began.

The Origin of Life

Miller and Urey theorized that over hundreds of millions of years, a variety of amino acids, fatty acids, and simple sugars built up in the warm oceans. Eventually, these compounds combined to form clusters called *coacervate droplets*. Many scientists believe that these clusters of organic molecules were the precursors of cells. Although they were not living organisms, they exhibited many of the characteristics of cells. For example, molecules at the edge of the cluster formed a protective coat much like a cell's membrane. The outer layer of each droplet shielded internal molecules from the surrounding environment. As time passed, the materials inside a few of the droplets somehow learned to function, grow, and reproduce as a single unit. In other words, they became living beings.

A number of recent discoveries cast doubt on this theory. In 1996, scientists announced the discovery of some microscopic fossils in Greenland. The microbes may have lived almost 3.9 billion years ago.

If these findings are accurate, it means that microscopic life-forms were alive soon after Earth's crust solidified. These hardy creatures somehow managed to survive frequent asteroid and comet impacts. It is estimated that these impacts generated enough heat to boil off a 9,800-foot (3,000-m)-deep ocean.[1] Apparently, life existed when Earth was still a treacherously hot place. This environment is nothing like the warm, stable ocean imagined by Miller and Urey.

What type of organism could live in this hot, acidic, carbon dioxide-rich environment? The answer seems clear—archaebacteria. Many scientists now agree that chemo-autotrophic archaebacteria—such as those living in Yellowstone National Park's Obsidian Pool, around hydrothermal vents on the ocean floor, or deep below Earth's surface—are similar to Earth's first inhabitants. The deep sea or rocks thousands of feet underground would have offered protection from all the forces upsetting the surface.

If the earliest life was chemoautotrophic, how did photoautotrophic organisms evolve? Why did photosynthesis become the dominant process for converting environmental energy into cell energy and food? If the earliest organisms did not require sunlight, why is it so important today? If life without light was originally the rule, why is it now the exception? These questions are not easy to answer.

PHOTOSYNTHESIS: HOW IT ALL BEGAN

Scientists do not yet know when, how, or why creatures evolved to depend on photosynthesis. "It is going to require 50 to 100 genomes, of organisms that are widely distributed throughout the universal tree of life, to really have a sense of what happened in our evolutionary history." says Mitch Sogin, a scientist at the Marine Biological Laboratory in Woods Hole, Massachusetts.[2]

For now, scientists are piecing together plausible explanations based on what they do know. As they learn more about organisms living at hydrothermal vents and in subterranean environments, the answers may become clearer. Here's one possible scenario for the development of photosynthesis and the evolution of early life.

Imagine that you are miles below the surface of an ocean on early Earth. Chemoautotrophic organisms cover every inch of a deep-sea chimney. They spend most of their time taking in hydrogen sulfide, carbon dioxide, and other substances spewing from the crack in the ocean floor. Most of the microbes do not have any way of sensing how close they are to the vent. Some drift too far from the temperate vent environment and freeze. Others move too close to the vent and fry.

A few of the microorganisms happen to have the ability to sense the soft glowing light emitted by the vent. They are extremely lucky. They have all descended from a microbe that experienced a genetic change so significant that it altered the course of life on Earth. The sequence of nucleotide bases in the DNA of this microbe's ancestors had been undergoing random changes for generations. When just the right change occurred in this microbe's DNA, it suddenly developed the ability to manufacture a protein that could trap photons of light given off by the vent. This ability was passed on to all of the microbe's descendants, so they were also able to judge their position relative to the vent. These microbes had a significant advantage over their neigh-

Little Things Make All the Difference

It may be difficult to believe that a few small changes in an organism's DNA could allow it to sense light given off by a hydrothermal vent. In fact, it is unlikely, improbable, and even practically impossible that a random genetic change will be so beneficial to an organism. But because these tiny changes are happening all the time, it's only a matter of time before the accumulated changes begin to make a difference.

This is what Darwin's theory of natural selection is all about. This is how giraffes developed long necks, how fish grew legs and came out onto land, and how humans developed the ability to reason. Darwin's evolutionary theory ultimately must explain the process by which some ancient eubacteria merged with archaebacteria in a symbiotic relationship. It must also demonstrate how these creatures developed into more advanced organisms called protoctists. Finally, it must show how protoctists evolved into plants, fungi, and animals.

bors. They were able to avoid freezing and frying, so they lived longer and produced more offspring.

As time passed, a few of the microbes drifted up from the dark depths of the ocean to shallow hot springs, which were also rich in sulfides. Some forms of life came into contact with sunlight for the first time. Since these microbes were already able to trap photons, all they had to do was develop a way to harness the captured energy. Eventually, a few microorganisms happened to undergo a series of genetic changes that allowed them to evolve a biochemical system that could use the Sun's rays to manufacture the materials they need to grow and reproduce.

This is probably about the time that the universal ancestor of every living thing alive today began to evolve in two separate directions. Some of its descendants continued to inhabit environments with plenty of hydrogen sulfide. Like their parent and their parent's parent, the descendants used chemosynthesis or methanogenesis to obtain the energy that powered their cellular activities. Today's archaebacteria, and possibly a few types of eubacteria, are the direct descendants of these creatures. Other descendants of the universal ancestor became increasingly dependent on photosynthesis. Their direct descendants include many of the eubacteria alive today.

Among the earliest photosynthesizers were the purple sulfur bacteria. They used hydrogen sulfide, not water, to carry out a type of photosynthesis that did not produce oxygen. At that time, hydrogen sulfide was released into the atmosphere by Earth's many active volcanoes. Purple sulfur bacteria were the first organisms to manufacture chlorophyll—the pigment that all green plants use to capture sunlight today.

Scientists believe that about 3 billion years ago some of these purple sulfur bacteria began to change. Eventually,

The Origin of Life

after many generations, the descendants of the purple sulfur bacteria—called cyanobacteria—began to use water rather than hydrogen sulfide for photosynthesis. Because water was much more plentiful than hydrogen sulfide on Earth's surface, cyanobacteria soon outnumbered purple sulfur bacteria.

Wherever there was water and sunlight, cyanobacteria flourished. Today, scientists have named more than 10,000 different kinds of these tiny photosynthesizers. They can be found in just about every imaginable terrestrial habitat where light and water abound.

As the cyanobacteria photosynthesized, they produced carbohydrates, which they used as food and a source of energy. They also released huge quantities of oxygen. After hundreds of millions of years, the cyanobacteria had released enough oxygen to completely saturate the world's oceans. As a result, oxygen began to escape into the atmosphere.

The cyanobacteria kept on growing and dividing. Soon the composition of the atmosphere began to change. As centuries and millenia passed, the amount of oxygen in the atmosphere continued to increase. At the same time, the quantity of carbon dioxide declined. Today, oxygen is the second most common component of the atmosphere. (Nitrogen is the most common.)

About 1.5 billion years ago, some kinds of eubacteria and archaebacteria fused to form more complex cells. Today, we call the new organisms that evolved from those fusions protoctists. They are the ancestors of plants, animals, and fungi. Fossils of early protoctists show that they were larger than bacteria. In the cells of ancient—and modern—protoctists are internal structures called organelles.

Eventually, the original protoctists gave rise to modern protoctists, such as slime molds and algae, as well as fungi, plants, and animals. According to Margulis and Schwartz, the chloroplasts and *mitochondria* in modern eukarya are the descendants of two kinds of eubacteria that joined forces with the earliest protists 2 billion years ago. Because the protists evolved from archaebacteria, certain protein molecules of modern archaebacteria resemble those of eukarya. This theory also explains why some RNA of archaebacteria is more similar to eukarya RNA (outside chloroplasts and mitochondria) than it is to the RNA of eubacteria.

LIFE MOVES ONTO LAND

The first marine invertebrates probably lived about 600 million years ago. They were thin, flat creatures that probably floated on the surface of the ocean. By 500 million years ago, the ancestors of most of the creatures alive today had evolved. The oldest *vertebrate* fossil is a fishlike animal that had thick bony plates, but no jaws.

Over the next 100 million years, life moved onto land. The first living things to populate the dry rocky surface were cyanobacteria and other soil bacteria as well as protoctists. By 450 million years ago, plants and fungi were living on land, too. These two groups helped each other stay wet in their new environment. Although plants, which had evolved from green algae, could conduct photosynthesis, they had trouble extracting nutrients from Earth's dry, rocky surface. Fungi had—and still have—the opposite problem. They can't photosynthesize, so they can't make their own food. They are, however, masters at absorbing minerals from rock. By living together, both types of organisms were able to survive on land.

Fungi invaded the root systems of plants. When they collected nutrients from rocks, they delivered some directly to the plants' root cells. Because the plants received nutrients, they were healthy. They could carry out photosynthesis and manufacture carbohydrates. The fungi fed on some of these carbohydrates. Over the next 80 million years, plants carpeted the surface of Earth.

At the same time that plants were stretching toward the far reaches of terrestrial Earth, the first animals crawled up onto land. These arthropods were very similar to modern scorpions. As time passed, natural selection wielded its magic wand. The result was insects—the largest, and most diverse, class of animals alive today.

In the meantime, life continued to develop in the oceans, too. About 350 million years ago, lobe-finned fish went through some very important changes. Their gills were replaced by lungs, and their fins developed into sturdy legs. The amphibians—the first vertebrates to live on land—came into being. Of course, these incredible changes happened very slowly—over millions of years. The mudskipper, which is still alive today, gives scientists a good idea of what the earliest amphibians were like. This small creature breathes through gills in the water and absorbs oxygen through the lining of its mouth when it's on land. Mudskippers spend their days scurrying across mudflats on their enlarged front fins.

As the eons ticked away, animals adapted in other ways to make life on land easier. They developed a new system for hearing; thick, watertight skin to prevent their precious body fluids from evaporating; and internal fertilization, so that there was no risk of sperm and eggs drying out and dying.

The first reptiles appeared about 320 million years ago. They were the dominant group of animals on Earth for the next 170 million years and eventually gave rise to the first flying vertebrates—the birds. About 230 million years ago, in the midst of the Age of Reptiles, the first mammals developed

from a group of small reptiles called the theraspids. Mammals did not change much until about 65 million years ago, when the dinosaurs mysteriously died out. Since then, the mammals have diversified rapidly to fill ecological niches previously occupied by dinosaurs. Today, there are about 4,500 species of mammals on Earth—one of them is human beings.

When mudskippers come onto land, they use their front fins like legs.

ONCE SHUNNED, NOW SALUTED

As you learned at the beginning of this chapter, no one is certain how life first arose on Earth. For many years, most scientists subscribed to the model proposed by Miller and Urey, even though it left many questions unanswered. Now that fossils in Greenland suggest that life existed on Earth

The Origin of Life

almost 4 billion years ago, scientists are looking at other scenarios for the origin of life. They are asking an important question: Where did the universal ancestor come from?

In the 1970s, Fred Hoyle and Chandra Wickramasinghe, astronomers at the University of Wales in Great Britain, offered an alternative explanation for life's origin. They suggested that life did not develop on Earth at all. Their controversial theory claimed that life had originated somewhere else in the solar system and traveled to Earth, perhaps on a meteoroid or comet.

According to this panspermia theory, the seeds of life were originally scattered throughout the solar system and thrived wherever conditions were right. When the planets first formed, Earth, Venus, and Mars had similar atmospheres and, in fact, all may have supported life for a while. As time passed, however, this changed. Because Mars is much smaller and colder than Earth, it's atmospheric pressure is much lower. As a result, most of its atmosphere drifted off into space. At the same time, all the carbon dioxide in Venus's atmosphere caused the planet to heat up. Today, the average temperature on Venus is about 800°F (430°C).

Scientists believe that both planets may have originally had water on their surfaces. Mars has features that appear to be ancient riverbeds and floodplains. There may have also been an ocean at one time. When the planet began to lose its atmosphere, the water evaporated and the vapor escaped into space along with other atmospheric gases. Many scientists believe that water still exists on Mars, as frozen crystals in the soil and as polar ice caps.

There is some evidence suggesting that the entire surface of early Venus was covered by an ocean. What happened to all this water? The answer may be a warning to us all. The carbon dioxide in the Venusian atmosphere trapped incoming solar radiation, just like the glass walls of

a greenhouse. A similar type of greenhouse effect may be responsible for global warming on Earth today.

In the end, it seems that the reason life thrives on Earth, but not on Venus, has everything to do with each planet's distance from the Sun. Because Earth is farther from the Sun than Venus, our planet has always received less solar energy than Venus. This slight difference gave the life in Earth's oceans a little more time to develop photosynthesis

Is Mars the original home of the universal ancestor of all life on Earth?

The Origin of Life

and start pumping vast quantities of oxygen into the oceans. Thus, in some senses, life saved itself.

Photosynthetic bacteria do not deserve all the credit, however. At the same time that they were oxygenating the world, the oceans were dissolving vast quantities of carbon dioxide. As you learned in Chapter 5, when carbon dioxide mixes with water, it is converted to carbonic acid. This weak acid reacted with rocks and formed carbonates. Today, Venus's atmosphere has about seventy times more carbon dioxide than Earth's. If, however, all the carbon dioxide tied up in Earth's carbonate rocks was suddenly released, the amount of carbon dioxide in the atmospheres of both planets would be about the same.

Jupiter's moon Europa may also have had an ocean at one time. In fact, some scientists think the ocean may still exist beneath the moon's icy surface. They claim that heat from deep within Europa prevents the ocean from turning into ice. If Europa has liquid water, could it also have life?

If life did originally exist on several worlds, where did it come from? How did it travel through space? And how did it end up on the worlds? In their book, *Diseases from Space*, Hoyle and Wickramasinghe argued that a bacterium is so small that it could fall to Earth without the atmosphere's friction causing it to heat up and vaporize. As evidence, they pointed out that a number of major meteor showers coincided with historic plagues.

Hoyle and Wickramasinghe were initially ostracized by the scientific community. Recently, however, growing numbers of scientists have begun to think that life on Earth may have extraterrestrial origins after all. Interestingly, the new research that has made many scientists reconsider the panspermia theory is nearly as controversial as the idea presented by Hoyle and Wickramasinghe 20 years ago.

"Meteorite Brings Martian Life to Earth"—it sounds like a headline from the *National Enquirer,* but it's not. On August 6, 1996, the National Aeronautics and Space Administration (NASA) issued a carefully worded statement announcing that a meteorite that crashed into Antarctica 13,000 years ago contains chemicals and structures that might have been created by Martian microbes 3.6 billion years ago. The incredible news quickly spread to every corner of the globe.

Since that day, scientists all over the world have been reanalyzing NASA's methods and data. A slew of papers contradict various aspects of the findings. Many others question the papers that cast doubt on the first one. When all is said and done, it cannot be denied that the potato-shaped meteorite does have three characteristics that suggest life—it was exposed to the right temperatures while on Mars, it has organic and mineral byproducts that could have been formed by microbes, and high-power microscopic images show wormlike structures that are similar to some types of terrestrial bacteria, only much smaller.

These tiny tubelike structures may be fossils of microorganisms that lived on Mars more than 3.6 billion years ago.

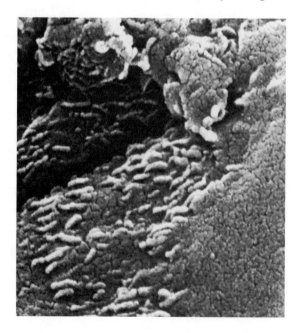

"Although there are alternative explanations for each of these phenomena when taken individually, when they are considered collectively, particularly in view of their special association, we conclude that they are evidence of primitive life on Mars," read the final sentence of the NASA team's report, which was published in the prestigious journal *Science.*

The Origin of Life

Unfortunately, this evidence is not convincing enough to prove that life once existed below the surface of Mars. We will not know for sure whether the meteorite really has signs of Martian life until scientists have more samples to study. Data collected by the Mars Pathfinder mission may provide just the information scientists need.

HOW COULD IT HAPPEN?

Scientists estimate that every year about 2 tons of Martian material rains down on Earth. Most of this matter burns up as it passes through Earth's protective shield—the atmosphere. Every now and then, however, a meteorite (any piece of material from space that lands on a planet's surface) hits Earth. By analyzing meteorites, scientists know that most are pieces of comets or asteroids that have traveled through space for millions of years before they are captured by Earth's gravitational field and pulled toward our planet.

Primitive Earth was bombarded by meteorites as well as entire comets and asteroids. Many scientists believe that these collisions brought important materials to Earth. Comets, which are balls of ice and rock, may have supplied the water that filled Earth's ancient oceans. Comets and asteroids may have also carried a variety of organic compounds, including amino acids, to Earth. Most scientists do not have trouble accepting such theories.

What they have more difficulty believing is that these extraterrestrial visitors might have brought living organisms to Earth. It is not, however, an impossible proposition. We know that some microbes can remain viable for millions of years, even without food.

Perhaps the common ancestor of archaebacteria and eubacteria—the creature that somehow managed to survive

Earth's fiery childhood—was tough enough to endure being dislodged from the Martian surface by an impact or explosion and then embarking on a daunting 10 million-year journey from Mars to Earth.

When asked about the hardiness of *Methanococcus jannaschii*, the archaebacteria sequenced by scientists in 1996, John N. Reeve, a microbiologist at Ohio State University in Columbus, said, "This organism is as good a candidate as you could get for something arriving on a Martian meteorite."

Did the first life arrive from Mars? Are all Earthlings actually Martians? Or did life actually exist on Earth first and then possibly travel to Mars? These and other questions have electrified the scientific community. If life did not develop on Earth, or on Mars, where did it come from? Is life a fairly ordinary phenomenon throughout the universe?

These are among the many questions that science has yet to answer.

Conclusion

Each day, each week, each month, each year scientists get closer to answering the question that has always been at the center of biology: What is life? This question seems simple enough, but don't be deceived. In order to provide a satisfactory answer, it is necessary to study our world, and perhaps others, closely. We must discover what all living beings have in common and the minimal requirements for survival. This knowledge will be incomplete until scientists can determine exactly when, where, and how Earth's earliest creatures developed.

Research conducted in the last few decades has shown time and again that life is highly adaptable and has relatively few absolute requirements. Not all life needs a temperate climate or oxygen or even a constant source of food. This book has considered whether light is necessary for life.

The creatures we know best—the plants and animals that inhabit the fields and forests of North America and Europe, the open plains of Africa, the rain forests of Earth's tropical regions, and the coral reefs and intertidal zones of the oceans—are, indeed, dependent on the Sun's rays. Sunlight energizes photosynthesis, which allows plants, algae, and many kinds of bacteria to convert carbon dioxide and water into carbohydrates and other materials they need to survive. When herbivores eat plants and carnivores eat herbivores, these materials are transferred to the animals' bodies. Photosynthesis also supplies the oxygen terrestrial organisms need to breathe.

Because photoautotrophs indirectly provide food to life in the deep ocean and caves, these creatures are dependent on sunlight. The organisms living around hydrothermal vents and underground aquifers also rely on the Sun. They need the oxygen produced by photosynthesis. The only ecosystems that appear to be completely independent of the Sun are located thousands of feet below Earth's surface. The communities of archaebacteria and eubacteria found inside hard igneous rock seem to require only hydrogen minerals in the rock and rainwater that has picked up carbon dioxide to produce the materials they need to live, grow, and reproduce. Studies conducted on these tiny creatures strongly suggest that there is, in fact, life without light on Earth. Whether similar creatures live on, or within, other planets remains to be seen.

Glossary

amphipod—a small animal that is closely related to pill bugs, shrimp, and crabs.

aquifer—a water-bearing layer of permeable rock, sand, or gravel.

archaebacteria—a group of bacteria that may be closely related to the first creatures on Earth.

autotroph—a creature that does not rely on other living things for food. See *heterotroph, photoautotroph,* and *chemoautotroph*.

bioluminescent—able to produce light.

biomass—the total amount of living matter on Earth.

bivalve—a group of mollusks with two shells—clams, mussels, and oysters.

black smoker—a deep-sea vent chimney that spouts a fountain of hot, black, sulfide-rich water.

buoyant—able to float on the surface of or at a certain depth of a liquid.

calcium carbonate—the chemical name for limestone.

carbohydrate—a compound used by living things as a source of energy. It is made of carbon, hydrogen, and oxygen.

carnivore—a meat-eating animal.

chemoautotroph—an organism that gets energy from a chemical source and does not rely on other living things for food. See *autotroph* and *chemoheterotroph*.

chemoheterotroph—an organism that gets energy from a chemical source and eats other living things to get the materials it needs to survive. See *autotroph, chemoautotroph,* and *heterotroph*.

chemosynthesis—the process by which microorganisms use the energy of chemical reactions to produce the materials they need to survive from carbon dioxide and water.

chlorophyll—the pigment in plants that captures energy from the Sun.

chloroplast—the cellular organelle that contains chlorophyll.

class—a group of organisms within a phylum that share characteristics.

coacervate droplet—a nonliving cluster of organic materials that may have developed into the first cell.

cold-blooded—having a body temperature that is not internally regulated. As a result, the organism's temperature varies with the temperature of its surrounding environment.

continental drift—the slow movement of the continents due to the changing position of the plates that make up the surface of Earth.

convection—the circular flow of heat through a substance in which some areas are warmer than others. Differences in density and gravitational force keep the fluid circulating.

core—Earth's innermost layer.

crust—Earth's outermost layer.

crustacean—a member of the group of animals that includes lobsters, crabs, shrimp, and amphipods.

cyanobacterium—a bacterium that has the ability to produce oxygen when it photosynthesizes.

decomposer—an organism the feeds on waste matter.

electromagnetic spectrum—the total range of electromagnetic radiation, from the longest wavelength radio waves to the shortest gamma rays. The spectrum also includes ultraviolet and infrared energy, visible light, X rays, and microwaves.

electron—a tiny particle that carries a negative charge and is present in all atoms. In an atom, the electrons move about a central nucleus made of protons and neutrons.

element—a substance that contains only one type of atom.

enzyme—a kind of protein that makes chemical reactions occur more quickly or at a lower temperature.

eubacteria—the collective term used to describe all bacteria except archaebacteria.

family—a group of organisms within an order that share characteristics.

food chain—the series of living creatures that consume one another. For example, an eagle might eat a sparrow that has eaten a grasshopper that fed on grass.

genome—all of the genetic material within an organism.

genus (plural **genera**)—a group of organisms within a family that share certain characteristics.

geyser—a spring that occasionally shoots off jets of water and steam.

hemoglobin—a bright red blood molecule that carries oxygen.

herbivore—an organism that eats only plants.

heterotroph—a creature that eats or absorbs carbon compounds from other organisms. See **autotroph, chemoautotroph,** and **chemoheterotoph**.

hot spring—any naturally occurring water heated by geothermal energy. A hot spring may be quiet, or it may erupt as a geyser.

hydrogen sulfide—one of the substances found in water spewed from hydrothermal vents on the ocean floor.

hydrothermal vent—a crack in the ocean floor that releases hot water containing a variety of minerals from which microbes can gain energy.

igneous rock—rock formed by the solidification of magma.

invertebrate—an animal that has no backbone.

ion—an atom or molecule that carries a positive or negative electrical charge.

kingdom—scientists divide the living world into five major groups called kingdoms. They are plants, animals, fungi, protoctists, and bacteria.

mantle—a thick layer of hot rock below Earth's crust.

marine snow—the remains of organisms that drift down from the sunlit surface waters of the ocean to the depths.

melanophore—a cell containing pigment bodies made of melanin.

methanogen—a type of archaebacteria that obtains energy from methane.

midocean ridge—the undersea mountain range that encircles Earth.

mitochondrion (plural **mitochondria**)—the cell organelle that derives energy from oxygen in eukarya. It probably evolved from a eubacterium.

natural selection—a theory proposing that organisms with more favorable mutations are more likely to survive and reproduce.

nucleotide base—one of the four building blocks of DNA: adenine (A), cytosine (C), thymine (T), and guanine (G).

omnivore—a creature that feeds on a combination of plants, animals, and other organisms.

order—a group of organisms within a class that share certain characteristics.

organic matter—material that contains carbon bound to hydrogen, often derived from living or dead organisms.

phylum (plural **phyla**)—a group of organisms within a kingdom that share certain characteristics.

photoautotroph—an organism that gets energy to make the materials it needs to survive from sunlight and does not rely on other living things for food. See **autotroph** and **chemoautotroph**.

photosynthesis (oxygen-producing)—the process by which green plants, algae, and cyanobacteria use energy from sunlight to make food from carbon dioxide and the hydrogen in water.

photosynthesis (non-oxygen producing)—the process by which purple sulfur bacteria and some other bacteria use sunlight to make food from carbon dioxide and the hydrogen in hydrogen sulfide.

planetesimal—one of many large bodies that formed from the accumulation of particles released when the universe formed. Some planetesimals became planets.

plates—large pieces of Earth's crust. There are six major plates and about a dozen smaller ones.

protist—one of the smallest protoctists. A protist consists of one cell or just a few cells.

protoctist—a eukoryote that cannot be classified as a plant, an animal, or a fungi. This group includes seaweed, slime molds, diatoms, and many other organisms.

polysaccharide—a complex carbohydrate, such as starch.

radiation—energy emitted in the form of waves or particles.

radioactive decay—the gradual loss of energy by elements in the form of alpha, beta, or gamma rays.

rift valley—the chasm that forms where two of Earth's plates are pulling apart.

seafloor spreading—the process of creating new seafloor as Earth's crust is pulled or pushed apart and magma moves up to fill the cracks.

sedimentary rock—rock that forms over time from erosion, transport, deposit, and hardening of seashells and sand.

seep community—an ecosystem that forms around cracks in the ocean floor. A seep forms at points where Earth's plates crash into each other, while hydrothermal vents form at places where plates are being pulled apart.

silica—the material from which quartz, sand, flint, and other white or colorless minerals are composed. It contains the elements silicon and oxygen.

solution cave—a cave formed over time by the dissolving action of underground water on sedimentary rock, such as limestone or gypsum.

species—a group of organisms within a genus that share certain characteristics. All members of a species can interbreed and produce healthy offspring.

speleologist—a scientists who studies caves.

stalactite—a pillarlike limestone structure that forms on the ceilings of caves.

stalagmite—a pillarlike limestone structure that builds up from the floors of caves.

subduction—the movement of one of Earth's plates under another.

symbiotic/symbiosis—a close association between two or more organisms of different species.

taxonomy—the system of identification, naming, and classification scientists use to show physical and behavioral similarities among living things.

terrestrial—of or relating to Earth. The term is used to refer to land surface on Earth or the other inner planets of our solar system.

troglobite—an organism that lives in the innermost regions of caves.

trophosome—an organ in giant tubeworms that contains chemosynthetic bacteria.

vertebrate—an animal that has a backbone. This group includes mammals, reptiles, amphibians, birds, and most fish.

visible light—the portion of the electromagnetic spectrum that is visible to humans.

water table—the top of the portion of the ground that is completely saturated with water.

Source Notes

CHAPTER TWO

1. Sylvia A. Earle. "The Frontier Below." *Scientific American Triumph of Discovery: A Chronicle of Great Adventures in Science.* New York: Henry Holt and Company, 1995, p. 155.

2. Cindy Lee Van Dover. *The Octopus's Garden: Hydrothermal Vents and Other Mysteries of the Deep Sea.* New York: Helix Books/Addison-Wesley Publishing Company, 1996, p. 7.

3. Robert D. Ballard. "The Ocean Depths." *The Ocean Realm.* Washington, D.C.: National Geographic Society, 1978, p. 151.

4. Cheryl Lyn Dybras. "The Deep Sea Floor Rivals Rain Forest in Diversity of Life." *Smithsonian,* January 1996, p. 96.

CHAPTER THREE

1. Van Dover, p. 125.

2. Van Dover, p. 129.

3. Victoria A. Kaharl. *Water Baby: The Story of Alvin.* New York: Oxford University Press, 1990, p. 229.

CHAPTER FOUR

1. Robert D. Ballard, *Explorations: My Quest for Adventure and Discovery Under the Sea.* New York: Alfred A. Knopf, 1996, p. 183.

2. Kaharl, 178–179.

3. Zimmer, Carl. "The Light at the Bottom of the Sea." *Discover,* November 1996, p. 64.

4. Van Dover, p. 134.

5. Van Dover, p. 57.

6. John Travis. "Live Long and Prosper." *Science News,* September 28, 1996, p. 201.

CHAPTER FIVE

1. Malcolm W. Brown. "Evolving in the Dark." *New York Times,* December 12, 1995, p. C1.

CHAPTER SIX

1. Elizabeth Pennisi. "Saving Hades' Creatures." *Science News,* March 13, 1993, p. 172.

2. Pennisi, p. 174.

3. Richard Monastersky. "Deep Dwellers: Microbes Thrive Far Below Ground." *Science News,* March 29, 1997, p. 193.

CHAPTER SEVEN

1. Virginia Morrell. "Microbiology's Scarred Revolution." *Science,* 2 May 1997, p. 701.

2. Elizabeth Culotta. "Life's Last Domain." *Science,* 23 August 1996, p. 1043.

3. Carl Zimmer. "Triumph of Archaea." *Discover.* February 1995, p. 30.

CHAPTER EIGHT

1. Morrell, p. 700.

2. John Travis. "Third Branch of Life Bares Its Genes." *Science News,* August 24, 1996, p. 116.

Resources

BOOKS

Ballard, Robert D. *Explorations: My Quest for Adventure and Discovery Under the Sea.* New York: Alfred A. Knopf, 1996.

Kaharl, Victoria A. *Water Baby: The Story of Alvin.* New York: Oxford University Press, 1990.

Margulis, Lynn and Dorian Sagan. *What Is Life?* New York: Simon & Schuster, 1996.

Rainis, Kenneth and Bruce Russell. *Guide to Microlife.* Danbury, CT: Franklin Watts, 1996.

Schaaf, Fred. *Planetology: Comparing Other Worlds to Our Own.* Danbury, CT: Franklin Watts, 1996.

Van Dover, Cindy Lee. *The Octopus's Garden: Hydrothermal Vents and Other Mysteries of the Deep Sea.* New York: Helix Books/Addison-Wesley, 1996. (This title was republished under the title *Deep-Sea Journeys.*)

INTERNET SITES

Follow scientists from the American Museum of Natural History, the University of Washington, and Pennsylvania State University as they explore the hydrothermal vents on the Juan de Fuca Ridge, which is off the coast of Washington and British Columbia.
http://www.ocean.washington.edu/outreach/revel

To find out more about the submersible *Alvin,* check out information on Woods Hole Oceanographic Institute's website.
http://www.marine.whoi.edu

The Edward's Aquifer Home Page has a number of diagrams showing its location and explaining how it formed. There are also photos of some of the creatures that have mysteriously appeared in local wells.
http://www.txdirect.net/users/eckhardt/intr.html

Scientists at the Lunar and Planetary Institute in Houston, Texas, present a thorough discussion of research performed on the Martian meteorite ALH84001 and the mysterious fossil-like material inside.
http://cass.jsc.nasa.gov/lpi/meteorites/
mars_meteorite.html

Index

About the Author

"Do you notice anything unusual about the trees in this part of the woods?" This is the question that launched Melissa Stewart into the world of science. When she was a child, she used to accompany her father and brother on long walks through the woods near their rural New England home.

One day, her father asked this question. She looked around and then sheepishly replied, "All the trees seem kinda small." He said she was right and asked if she knew why. When she seemed confused, her father explained that there had been a fire in the area about 25 years earlier. All the trees and other plants had been destroyed in the fire, but new ones had begun sprouting the very next spring.

"This experience taught me two things," says Stewart. "First, death is a natural part of life and the natural world is so powerful that it can regenerate itself. Second, by looking around and noticing things, you can actually learn a lot about an area's natural history. I was hooked. Ever since that moment, I have wanted to know everything about the natural world."

Stewart grew up in Southampton, Massachusetts, and now lives in Danbury, Connecticut. She earned a B.S. in biology from Union College in Schenectady, New York and an M.A. in science journalism from New York University in New York City. "I chose this path because I didn't want to limit myself," says Stewart. "I didn't want to spend my entire life doing research in just one area. Now I get paid to learn everything I can about every area of science."